3+ 3,40

HISTORICAL INTERPRETATIONS and AMERICAN HISTORIANSHIP

by

Jennings B. Sanders

THE ANTIOCH PRESS · 1966

To My Wife
MARY PURVIANCE SANDERS

CONTENTS

HISTORICAL INTERPRETATIONS
AND AMERICAN HISTORIANSHIP

INTRODUCTION

THE OBJECT of this book is threefold: to examine what historians, philosophers, and other scholars have said about the nature, meaning, and purpose of history; to analyze the current status of historianship, with special reference to the craft in the United States; and to venture an interpretation of American history. The book makes no effort to develop themes of historical method and historiography. On these subjects there are already several satisfactory works in print.

"It should be known," wrote Ibn Khaldûn of Tunis (1332–1406), "that history is a discipline that has a great number of approaches." [1] The "great number of approaches" to history [2] have made its study at once fascinating and troublesome, and with some scholars thinking about history has absorbed more attention and energy than writing history itself. Thus, Georg W. F. Hegel, more celebrated as a philosopher than as a historian, noted that each historian tries to be "original" in method and "individual" in viewpoint. "Instead of writing history," said Hegel, "we are always beating our brains to discover how history ought to be written." [3]

A search for "laws" of history has also long been an interest of historians and philosphers. The nineteenth-century English historian Henry Thomas Buckle, [4] noting the recurrence of certain phenomena within a limited space-time complex, arrived at a belief in the predictability of the future. And in our own country, the late Professor Edward P. Cheyney, [5] of the University of Pennsylvania, formulated what he was convinced were "laws of history." Because of the variables involved, however, most historians have disbelieved in the predictability of the future and in the existence of "historical laws." For as economist John Maynard Keynes demonstrated, there are perils in predicting from "a percentage of happenings" without an analysis of "the circumstances accompanying the individual instances. . . ." [6] Nevertheless, it is a striking fact, and one which shows that interest in historical philosophy is not limited to academic circles, that recently an advertizing executive was so impressed by Buckle's theories of predictability that he made the English historian's work required reading for his staff.[7]

But one may have a philosophy or theory of history and believe that it offers some helpful clues to the past and to the future, without believing that it operates as a law. For instance, if the word "interests" be interpreted to include both the material and the spiritual, one might say that men usually act in accordance with what they believe to be their interests. And one might also say that, in addition to this universal principle, men in different parts of the world develop different outlooks and cultural patterns which give character to their own history.

On the basis of these views, the author has formulated a theory of American history. And while he recognizes that any single interpretation of a nation's history necessarily has limitations, he believes that the theory advanced is a valid interpretation of the American past. In any event, he trusts that it may stimulate thought and discussion about the meaning of American history, and that the book in its entirety may have a similar result for history in general.

I

HISTORY AND ITS
PHILOSOPHIC-SCIENTIFIC SETTING

A STUDY OF PHILOSOPHY is at once a necessity and a hazard for
the historian—a necessity because some of the best thinking about
history and its meaning has been done by philosophers, and a
hazard because philosophical writing often is more confusing than
illuminating. "What philosophy has lacked most of all," wrote
Henri Bergson, is "precision." "Philosophical systems," he said,
"are not cut to the measure of the reality in which we live; they
are too wide for reality." [1] Yet both precision and reality are important to historianship. In a vein somewhat similar to that of
Bergson, G. J. Renier, professor of Dutch history at the University
of London, believes that the admission of philosophy to history
would add to history confusion and uncertainty.[2] And Shailer
Mathews warned that "when a historian enters into metaphysics
he has gone to a far country from whose bourne he will never
return a historian." [3] Perhaps it was a fear of some such fate that
caused University of California historian Frederick J. Teggart to
conclude that the historian "must face his own problems" without
help from philosophers and scientists.[4]

PHILOSOPHY, HISTORY, AND MAN

But while the historian, like all specialists, must take care not to
lose himself in the auxiliary subjects related to his field of interest,
at the same time he cannot afford to ignore these allied disciplines.
For as Ernst Bernheim long ago pointed out, history's concern
is with man's development and is therefore related to such subjects

as philology, politics, sociology, philosophy, anthropology, and ethnology.[5] And since history's subject is man, the thinking about man by philosophers from earliest days down to recent existentialists, comes within his purview. Even novelists and dramatists, such as Tolstoy, O'Neill, and Sartre, who have thought deeply about life and the soul, have relevance for the historian's studies.

As more than one student has concluded, history is, in a sense, a vast epic in which every human being has a part—an epic enacted on a stage so huge that only an all-encompassing eye could comprehend it. The historian cannot take a place of vantage in the gallery the better to behold the pageant, for he, like other mortals, is himself in the midst of the play. Consequently, his descriptions of events from direct observation are limited by what he can see while performing his own part. Unlike most of the other players, however, the historian studies accounts made by observers who preceded him, and he tries to understand from these accounts and from his own observations how the play began, what scenes have preceded his own, and whither the play is tending. He knows that the play is multiform, ranging from the depths of tragedy to the heights of comedy. For even within the narrow compass of his particular part of the stage, he has witnessed these scenes and likely as not has been an actor in them.

Whatever man does, he does in time and space. While concepts of time and space may be illusions of the finite mind, the historian, in order to do his work, must accept them as realities. It is sometimes said that man moves from the past to the present, and into the future. Actually, man never lives in the past or the future, not even for a fraction of a second. He lives in the present only, and he cannot think the word before the present has become the past. The real present is so fleeting that it is but an infinitesimal part of the "specious present" that we have created for ourselves—a present that includes much of the past, as when we speak of the "present time," the "present generation," or the "present century." [6]

Concepts of the *historic present* and the *time present* are often confused. Karl R. Popper has said that the present is "the future of the past." [7] This, of course, can be true of the historic present only, not of the time present. For if time, like electric current, is instantaneously and completely used up, active past time is unthinkable and it cannot become or produce anything.

The flow of time is *from* the future, not into the future, and is fantastically rapid. In an effort to make time comprehensible, man has geared it down to slow movement. It is often remarked that in terms of planetary time, the period of man's existence on earth—saying nothing of the much briefer period of his recorded history—may be the equivalent of less than one minute of the twenty-four hour day. In terms of cosmic time, it would be even less—a mere flash. For time, as noted, seems not to be a static or slow-motion something through or with which we move, but an incredibly fast something that flows in upon us and gives us an infinite number of fleeting times-present in which we enact history. When we write history, therefore, we work with the symbols and the records of previous times-present. From these symbols and records we try to reconstruct not the past, but rather the present as it existed for a portion of humanity, say in the year 1000, 1815, or 1910; and we repeat the process for successive years until we reach the actual present.

HISTORY AND SCIENCE: PRE-RANKE ERA

During the past century, much of the philosophical controversy concerning history centered on or derived from the question: Is history a science? The question is twofold, involving both content and method. Most historians probably agree that the historical method is scientific—that is, that it is primarily inductive and thus proceeds from the particular to the general, not the reverse. But the larger assumption that history is a science which operates in accordance with laws and therefore comparable to physical science has not gained general acceptance by historians.[8] It is an assumption much more common among sociologists; indeed, Auguste Comte, the French philosopher who founded sociology, was one of the earliest scholars in the Western world to espouse the idea.

The belief that history is a science in that its methods are scientific first came to fruition in the Western world in modern Germany. But this conception of history, with its implicit doctrine of objectivity, reaches back to antiquity. Thus, Thucydides, historian of the Peloponnesian War, is sometimes referred to as the father of scientific history, much as Herodotus is regarded as the father of narrative history. Despite the placing of his own words as speeches in the mouths of some of the characters in his history, it must be said that, while the practice was indefensible by modern standards, it was not as reprehensible in the case of Thucydides as one might suppose. Thucydides informed his readers that while he heard some of the speeches, others he "got from various quarters" and that his own words represented what he thought was demanded of the speakers "by the various occasions. . . ." Moreover, Thucydides tested his sources and was concerned primarily with producing an exact account that would be useful for an understanding of the future. His history was not written "to win the applause of the moment, but as a possession for all time." [9]

Writing some five hundred years after Thucydides, the aristocratic and cynical Roman historian Tacitus likewise exhibited for his time marked skill and integrity in the handling of historical materials. Although in the matter of speeches he indulged a practice similar to that of Thucydides, Tacitus nevertheless in his *Annals* and *History* and other writings on his age and times showed remarkable analytical and narrative powers.[10]

Of medieval historians, the Cluniac monk Ordericus Vitalis was, for all his deficiencies, one of the best. Born of an English mother and a French father, Ordericus regarded himself as English. His great work, which occupied him for some eighteen years, was *The Ecclesiastical History of England and Normandy*. Stationed for over a half-century in the monastery of St. Evroul in Normandy, Ordericus had access to important sources for his history, and he was also in the mainstream of travel which brought him into contact with other scholarly minds. He himself traveled widely in England and France and thus was able to write of many conditions from first-hand observation. The *History* abounds in inaccuracies, repetitions, and faulty chronology, faults not especially surprising when it is remembered that the work reached back to early Christianity and was written within the "frame of reference" of a pious monk.

But Ordericus was not a servile copier, and his frankness in describing evils in the Church of his day is quite remarkable. Vice and other forms of worldliness abounded among both the regular and secular clergy of the twelfth century, and to these features of the Church, Ordericus would not close his eyes. For instance, after describing the worldly doings of the Bishop of Lisieux, our historian tells us that he "could write more about him, but I check my pen," since he wished to be fair and to tell of the Bishop's good as well as his foul deeds.[11]

Ordericus's treatment of social conditions during his time would alone be sufficient to give his *History* high rank. For whether it is forms of gambling, the affectation of wearing shoes with toes turned up like rams' horns, men's allegedly effeminate hair styles, or the state of medicine and learning, Ordericus is refreshingly vivid and instructive. "It is," wrote R. W. Church of the *History,* "as lively as real life, and also as confused and unassorted." [12] As for the latter qualities, perhaps Ordericus, like John Bach McMaster in writing the history of the American people, could have said that his account of social conditions was necessarily "confused and unassorted" because social life was that way.[13] One of the leading authorities on Norman history, Charles H. Haskins, has written that Ordericus's *History* was "the chef d'oeuvre of Norman historiography and the most important historical work written in France in the twelfth century." [14] Perhaps this was the worldly praise (his first object in writing was to achieve his personal salvation) Ordericus would have welcomed. For he wrote that, while he was not so situated as to be able to write of ancient times, "I labour, by God's help, to unfold with truth contemporary events for the instruction of posterity,—both such as have passed under my own observation, and those which, occurring in neighbouring countries, have come to my knowledge." [15]

The Renaissance era, noted for the critical spirit it engendered, produced more than one scholar who applied standards of the new learning to ancient writings. And yet it was not a European, but the Arabic scholar Ibn Khaldûn who, in the opinion of Arnold J. Toynbee, produced the greatest philosophy of history, not only of his time but of all time.[16] Khaldûn had competence in history and in what nowadays would be called the "auxiliaries of history." And he understood the principal sources of historical error and the chief rules of criticism.[17]

But most important for historiography was the advance in natural science and philosophy during the century between 1550 and 1650. Already Nicolaus Copernicus had given men a new and revolutionary concept of their world by showing that, contrary to the ancient Ptolemaic theory, the earth was not the center of the solar system with the sun revolving about the earth, but a system in which the earth and its sister planets revolved about the sun.

The great Polish astronomer's announcement was followed by the work of the German, Johan Kepler, who worked out the mathematics of the solar system and the elliptical orbits in which the different members of the system moved. And the Italian Galileo, through experimentation, discovered laws of falling bodies. The philosophical capstone for the new science was supplied by Francis Bacon and Frenchman René Descartes, who, departing from the long-accepted *deductive system* of reasoning from the general to the particular, insisted that just the reverse order (*inductive system*) was the way to truth.

The application of the new approach to the study of society was not long delayed. Italian psychologist and scientist Giovanni Battista (Giambattista) Vico (1668–1744) conceived of a science of society,[18] and has been credited with doing for his field of study what Descartes had done for natural science. It was Vico, says R. G. Collingwood, who laid "the foundation of the modern philosophy of history" and supplied to historical study the necessary ingredients of skepticism and critical judgment in examining documents.[19] "In the strict and critical sense," says Benedetto Croce, "historicism in the nineteenth century has only one true and proper precursor: Giambattista Vico. . . ." [20]

The promise of a critical scholarship which the Renaissance evoked was in considerable part defeated by the Reformation and the bitterly biased ecclesiastical writing it called forth. Then followed a period of rationalistic revolt, but, with the exception of the pioneer work of Vico, without any deepening of critical scholarship. Professor George P. Gooch has indicated that three forces operative at the turn of the nineteenth century were responsible for the rise of the modern critical historical scholarship commonly said to be "scientific." The first two of these forces were romanticism and nationalism; the third was the publication by Friedrich August Wolf of his *Prolegomena to Homer*.[21] The Romanticists, while accomplishing but little in pure historical scholarship, reversed the long-felt dislike of the past and showed how arresting and instructive a study of the past could be. Nationalism, called forth by the Napoleonic Wars, deepened the study of national origins and growth, and encouraged national pride. And Wolf's work, as noted below, set new canons for critical scholarship.

This new scholarship found its first distinguished representative in Barthold Georg Niebuhr, of the University of Bonn, who injected into Roman historical studies a critical approach they had never before enjoyed. To Niebuhr, the present could be understood only through understanding the past, and the past in turn must be approached from a thorough study of present-day institutions.

HISTORY AND SCIENCE: RANKE AND THE POST-RANKE ERA

But important as Niebuhr undoubtedly was, his work suffered from the author's resort to intuition when facts were lacking. For this reason, the authentic founder of modern historianship, sometimes called by the vague and unsatisfactory term *historismus,* or historicism, was not Niebuhr but Leopold von Ranke, of the University of Berlin. Author of over three-score volumes, including a history of the popes and works on Germany and other European countries, Ranke was the "patron saint" of the American historical profession at the turn of the twentieth century and was made an honorary member of the American Historical Association founded in 1884.* In the opinion of George P. Gooch, Ranke produced "a larger number of first-rate works than any historian who ever lived." [22]

Ranke claimed he had no prepossessions and that he approached historical investigations with an open mind. It was not his purpose, he said, to sit in judgment upon the past or provide lessons for the future; he would simply examine the records and tell exactly what had happened: *"Ich will nur sagen wie es eigentlich gewesen ist."* Actually, for all his vast learning, Ranke fell short of the goal he had set for himself. To tell exactly what had happened would have required a study of all segments of the life of countries whose history he wrote. But the Berlin professor was not concerned with *Kulturgeschichte;* his interest was *Staatengeschichte, or political history.*[23] Moreover, even within these limits, Ranke has been severely criticized[24] (in America, notably by Charles A. Beard) for failing to come to grips with highly controversial questions and for writing history largely from a conservative standpoint. As for objectivity, Beard and some other critics have maintained that complete objectivity such as that claimed by Ranke is unattainable and that it is impossible to write *"wie es eigentlich gewesen ist."* Beard contended that Ranke wrote subjectively and

* See below, p. 15.

that this was, in fact, the only way he could have written.[25] As Carl Becker observed: "Even the most disinterested historian has at least one preconception which is the fixed idea that he has none." [26]

Significant as they were for modern historianship, the canons of research represented by German scholarship in the nineteenth century did not originate with historians. As Charles Kendall Adams wrote in 1889: "The modern scientific study of history everywhere has a taproot running down into philology." [27] Adams mentioned especially Friedrich August Wolf, of the University of Halle, whose *Prolegomena to Homer* (1795) set new standards of criticism for both philology and history. This book, said Irish-born John Bagnell Bury in his inaugural address in 1903 as professor of history at Cambridge, was "one of a half-dozen which in the last three hundred years have exercised most effective influence upon thought." He said that the work "gave historians the idea of a systematic and minute method of analysing their sources, which developed into the microscopic criticism, now recognized as indispensable." To Bury, history, informed and guided by the new scholarship, was "simply a science, no less and no more." [28] Leopold von Ranke began his own career as a teacher of classical languages and of linguistic history.[29] It was Wolf's seminars at Halle that Ranke in 1830 adopted as the example for his own advanced history students. "To the teacher of history," said Adams, this event "was the beginning of a new epoch." [30]

THE HISTORY-AS-SCIENCE CONCEPT IN AMERICA

When Swiss historian Eduard Fueter in 1911 published his *Geschichte der Neuren Historiographie,* he devoted but four of his some six hundred pages of text to American historians. The four selected for notice were George Bancroft, John L. Motley, Francis Parkman, and William H. Prescott. These were the only American historians who had attained an international reputation, and it may be supposed that this was Fueter's reason for including them in a work treating modern historical writing. And yet the omission of so many names that, by the turn of the century, had become important in American historiography leaves the work highly deficient even as an outline, as it affects this country. For when Fueter wrote, Henry Adams had done his greatest work, McMaster had published most of his history, Channing had launched his magnum opus, and most of the volumes of the American Nation Series had appeared. Nor were Fueter's appraisals of the four historians selected very discerning. For instance, a judgment on lack of bias[31] surely could have been reached, especially in the case of Bancroft and Motley, only by making much of their research industry as indicated by scholarly notes and making little of the contents of their histories.

The scientific revolution of the seventeenth and eighteenth centuries, especially the discoveries in physics by Sir Isaac Newton, had turned the minds of economists and students of society toward possibilities of discovering comparable laws in social science. And following publication of Charles Darwin's evolutionary hypothesis in 1859, society came to be widely regarded, even among historians, as an organism which could be understood only by processes of dissection and by observance of evolutionary growth. Moreover, many Americans, especially those who in one way or another came to occupy rungs on the economic ladder considerably higher than those of their fellowmen, adopted the premises of "social Darwinism" [32] that natural selection and the survival of the fittest obtained among men in their economic and social relationships as well as among the lower species in their physical development. Professor William Graham Sumner, of Yale, became something of a high priest of the new philosophy which afforded John D. Rockefeller and others who had emerged on top in the rough and tumble of economic competition an easy and satisfying explanation, if not justification, of their success.

But in the United States, even before the Civil War, the limitations and problems of social science were succinctly stated by Charles Carey, who recognized man, "the molecule of society," as the new science's proper subject for study. Noting that "social science can scarcely be said to have an existence," Carey observed that chemistry, physics, and physiology underlay the science of man and the laws governing him.[33] More significantly, Lester Frank Ward, contrary to Englishman Herbert Spencer's view of static society, advanced the doctrine of a dynamic sociology. Ward identified, to his own satisfaction at least, social-economic laws, beginning with the "fundamental" one "that all men will, under all circumstances, seek their greatest gain." He wrote also of "the Law of Acquisition" and "the Law of Force." [34]

Among the earliest American historians, as distinguished from sociologists, to proclaim the applicability of scientific methods to history were Richard Hildreth (1807–1865) and John William Draper (1811–1882). Influenced by Newtonian physics and by the utilitarianism of Jeremy Bentham, Hildreth said that he would "apply to the philosophy of man's nature the same inductive method which has proved so successful in advancing what is called natural philosophy." [35] But his historical writing, alas, failed to attain the objectivity which employment of the scientific method was supposed to make possible. Draper, who was a versatile scholar, was professor of chemistry at the University of New York and a writer on physiology. Despite the apparent remoteness of these interests from historical studies, he also wrote a history of the American Civil War and a work on the intellectual history of Europe. "Social advancement," said Draper," is as completely under the control of natural law as is bodily growth." It was his view that "the civilization of Europe has not taken place fortuitously, but in a definite manner, and under the control of natural law. . . ." [36]

Much American historical writing during the last quarter of the nineteenth century fairly bristled with the words "science" and "scientific" and related terms. Thus, George Bancroft in his presidential address before the American Historical Association at their third annual meeting (1886), said that "the character of science attaches to our pursuits";[37] and Herbert Baxter Adams, who held the doctorate from Heidelberg, where his specialty had been political science more than history, and who taught by the German seminar method at Johns Hopkins University, had no doubt of history's scientific quality. In a work published in 1887, he wrote of "the scientific sessions of the seminary" at Hopkins and of seminaries at Harvard, Cornell, Michigan, and a few other American universities, "all individually ambitious . . . for the common cause of science." He hoped that state and municipal documents would "be represented in the scientific collection" of Hopkins, whose seminaries "are laboratories where books are treated like mineralogical specimens, passed about from hand to hand, examined and tested." [38] Even before the introduction of the seminar method at Hopkins by Dr. Austin Scott, assistant to George Bancroft, Henry Adams and his students at Harvard had employed methods of German historical scholarship.[39]

The extent to which the scientific conception of history had gained influence in American historical circles in the latter part of the nineteenth century was indicated by the worshipful attitude taken by the newly organized American Historical Association toward Leopold von Ranke. It was in 1885, at the Association's second meeting, that Ranke was voted his honorary membership, the first of its kind in the Association. The resolutions on this membership and the letter to Ranke from George Bancroft, President of the Association, are revealing.

> *Whereas:* The American Historical Association is deeply sensible of the debt which historical science owes to its oldest and most distinguished living exponent; and is desirous of signalizing its own devotion to pursuits which Leopold von Ranke has so conspicuously followed,

> *Resolved:* That the President of the Association be requested to transmit to that historian its first testimonial of honorary membership.[40]

In his letter to Ranke, Bancroft let idolatry have full sway:

> We wish for your benediction; and for that end we ask you, and, as yet, you alone, to accept the proof of our reverence by consenting to become our honorary member. We have meant to make this a special homage to yourself as the greatest living historian.[41]

The centennial of the great historian's birth was commemorated by an address by Professor E. G. Bourne at the Association's annual meeting in 1895.[42]

The *American Historical Review* was launched in 1895, and its very first article, a contribution by Professor William M. Sloane, had much to say about history as a science. It called attention to a "supposed feebleness of contemporary historical writing" and to the fact that critics regarded an "unscientific method" as one of the causes of this unfortunate state of affairs. "The real merit of the evolutionary philosophy which has captured the thought of our day," said the author, "lies in the fact that it has made possible a science of the humanities." To him, history was both scientific and democratic.[43]

Although he was not the first to do so, Henry Adams was one of the earliest American historians to seek in physical science a pattern of law in history. For historians, said Adams, "the single interest is the law of reaction between force and force—between mind and nature—the law of progress." [44] Adams had expressed the belief in 1884 that within another generation democratic society would permit psychology, physiology, and history to "join in proving man to have as fixed and necessary development as that of a tree. . . ." [45] Ten years later, he thought a science of history would come about in another fifty years, but that it would do no good.[46] He was certain that any law of history that might evolve would offend powerful interests and institutions—the church, state, capital, and labor.[47] In 1902 he was writing that science was to bring about a "cosmic collapse"—that "we are like monkeys, monkeying with a loaded shell. . . ."[48]

In a significant book entitled *The Law of Civilization and Decay: An Essay on History,* Brooks Adams, brother of Henry, claimed for himself the detachment of a scientist. His essay, he said, was free "from any preconceived bias. All theories . . . in the book . . . are the effect, and not the cause, of the way in which the facts unfold themselves. I have been passive." Adams stated that, as a "scientific observer," an author might suggest a law if facts seemed to justify one, "but to approve or disapprove of it would be as futile as to discuss the moral bearings of gravitation." He surveyed history from the Romans to modern times, emphasizing the role of money and the economy in affecting change, and the part of "barbaric blood" and blood of conquered peoples in strengthening the conqueror. He was of opinion that economic and scientific predominance in a society made for cultural decay and that highly centralized societies tended to disintegrate "under the pressure of economic competition. . . ." [49]

Although, as noted, historians have been less inclined than sociologists to admit the existence of laws in man's history, Edward P. Cheyney, professor of history at the University of Pennsylvania, identified several principles or tendencies which he designated "laws of history." These were a law of continuity, a law of democracy, a law of impermanence or mutability, a law of interdependence, a law of moral progress, and a law of necessity for free consent. These were laws, said Cheyney, which we would have to accept whether we wished to do so or not; they were "laws to be accepted and reckoned with as much as the laws of gravitation, or of chemical affinity, or of organic evolution, or of human psychology." [50]

But confident as Cheyney was about his "laws," these have not been accepted by most historians. With the possible exception of continuity and of impermanence or mutability, they have seemed at best suggestive and interpretive only.[51]

In a thoughtful book, Ernest Cuneo has recently applied scientific terms to some well-known historical developments and has formulated several "laws" (the "Law of Accession to Superior Energy," for example) to help explain humanity's past. He does not claim to have explained all history in terms of science, but only that such an explanation is possible. In his view, there is no hope that man can control his fate if there are no laws to guide him. This seems to suggest that man is expected to control his fate in some absolute way, and therefore that ascertainable laws must exist for his guidance.[52] This, however, is but one way of viewing the problem. May it not be that laws of history, if any, are beyond human comprehension, and that, for this reason, man is destined to control his fate with something less than scientific precision?[53]

SOME HISTORICAL INTERPRETATIONS
IN REVIEW

ALTHOUGH George M. Trevelyan said that no philosophy could be "extracted" from history and that he found none in it, he nevertheless believed that history's purpose was to instruct and inspire.[1] Since, in the broadest sense, whatever one thinks about history is a philosophy of history, perhaps even Trevelyan in his analysis of the nature and end of history makes himself a member of the philosophical circle. For history is as varied and as complex as life, and a multitude of interpretations inevitably flow from contact with the subject whether it is being investigated by the research student or merely being read for pleasure by the layman. As James A. Froude observed, history is like a child's box of letters from which any word can be spelled and any philosophy of history constructed.[2]

CHAOS, PROVIDENCE, AND RELIGION

Much philosophizing about history springs from two extreme positions: one, a belief that the life of humanity is and always has been a chaos and that things "just happen," the other, a belief that there is some kind of order in human events, however well or ill-understood this order may be. The concept of chaos has always posed intellectual problems, because it runs counter to what seems to be an established order in the physical universe. Many men have doubted that the cosmic pattern could be so irrational as to allow man to operate on a free-will basis—and man is free, says José Ortega Y Gasset, "whether I wish it or not" [3]—while at the same time compelling the physical world to operate in accordance with

law. The apparent conflict between ideas of law and free will under-
lies much of man's thinking about the meaning of history.

One of the oldest and most persistent historical interpretations
embraces both the chaotic and legalistic concepts just mentioned.
This is the Providential interpretation, or the view that nothing
"just happens"—that God is back of it all. According to this view,
it matters not at all whether happenings appear to finite-minded
man to be orderly or chaotic; for what seems chaotic to man may
be only a minute phase of a Providential and orderly plan so vast
as to be incomprehensible to the human mind. This was the conclusion reached by Count Leo Tolstoy in his efforts to understand
the Napoleonic Wars. Tolstoy believed that only a knowledge of
the motivations of every participant in an event could explain it. He
recognized that such knowledge lay beyond the human ken, and
found himself obliged, therefore, to look to the laws of God. These
laws,[4] being of God's own making, God could modify or set aside
according to His will.

In the Providential sense, nothing is accidental or freakish.
For, as Maimonides put it, God "is the author of the generalities
as well as of the particulars. . . ."[5] A shell bursts and a fragment
of it instantly kills a soldier who had stepped into his fatal position
only a second before: the shell-burst was in accordance with physical law; the fragment was released in the particular way it was and
went to its mark, in accordance with physical law; and the soldier
was killed by the impact because a delicately balanced human
mechanism, operating in accordance with law, was disrupted. All
happened in accordance with Providential laws which were neither
modified nor suspended. While many persons believe that laws
operate in the affairs of men as well as among the stars and planets
and their atomic components, it is not so generally agreed that
there is a cosmic force, which some men choose to call God, having
power to modify or set aside these laws. Those who believe that
there is no power to manipulate laws of the universe insist that
when conditions are "right" for a thing to happen, it happens, and
there can be no stopping it.

Some persons who have reflected on the meaning of the world
and of man have become fatalists. In our own day, some of the
existentialists —and existentialist beliefs range all the way from
atheism to orthodox Christianity—while agreeing that man has
free will, argue that it is the free will of a man in a chaotic world,

and that whether he chooses to do right or wrong matters but little. The alleged nothingness of things, which is made so much of by some present-day existentialists, is an old theme reaching far back of their time, and it has been espoused by a variety of authors. Thus, Tolstoy has one of his leading characters musing "on the nothingness of greatness, on the nothingness of life . . . and on the nothingness . . . of death." [6] And Eugene O'Neill, in his *Long Day's Journey into Night,* suggests strongly the helplessness of man in the face of inexorable forces. Life, says his principal character, does cruel things to people, and people are helpless to prevent them; and one unpreventable thing leads to another, and so to final tragedy. Perhaps only in Anatole France's conception of men and their destiny is there struck a more tragic note: "They were born, they suffered, and they died." [7] And Voltaire saw history as "little else than a long succession of useless cruelties," [8] a pessimistic view comparable to Edward Gibbon's statement that history "is little more than the register of the crimes, follies and misfortunes of mankind." [9]

But many other persons have seen the universe, not as an unfriendly force making for human misery, but a force which, if understood, is capable of making for unlimited human happiness. Admitting the existence of laws by which men and the world are governed, these persons insist that man's duty is to seek an understanding of laws, and, understanding them, govern himself accordingly. To individual man, therefore, the world is beneficent or malevolent, depending upon his adaptation to the world's rules.

In the Western world, from Saint Augustine forward, some scholars have seen in history the working out of the Divine purpose in terms of Christianity. Theologians and philosophers, such as Bishop of Meaux Jacques Bénigne Bossuet (1627–1704), Jonathan Edwards (1703–58) and Georg Wilhelm Friedrich Hegel (1770–1831), regarded the birth of Christ as the focal point in history, the point toward which all previous history moved and from which all later history evolved. The view is not without its present-day advocates. In December, 1948, Professor Kenneth Scott Latourette of Yale devoted his presidential address before the American Historical Association to the Christian understanding of history, an understanding to which the speaker personally subscribed. The course of history was viewed by Latourette as God's search for man that He may transform him and save him.[10]

But the Christian interpretation of history has been sharply challenged. Thus, Karl Jaspers, himself a deeply religious man, holds that the Christian interpretation can be valid for Christian believers only, and therefore a different historical "axis" must be found. Jaspers moved the "axis of history" backward by several centuries from Christ's birth, in an effort to formulate a "schema of total conception" and to find an axial period more representative of world culture. This period, he believed, was 800–200 B.C., or "around 500 B.C.," when important intellectual and cultural advances were being made in China, India, Persia, and Greece, as well as in Palestine. No less than thinkers whom he criticizes, however, Jaspers believes in the unity of history and that it moves "from the One to the One"; it is only on the selection of an "axial period" not exclusively Christian that he differs from them.[11]

Of especial relevance to the religious interpretation of history in our day is *A Study of History* by Arnold J. Toynbee. Although one distinguished reviewer of this work concludes that, to Toynbee, history is the process by which "God becomes man in Christ," [12] it is easy to err in identifying Toynbee too closely with Christianity. For while the Christian emphasis is dominant in Toynbee's work, it is by no means an exclusive emphasis. There is in his *Study* a large degree of religious eclecticism, embracing Christianity, Confucianism, Hinduism, and Mohammedanism. Presumably in agreement with Jaspers on the point, Toynbee sees history as "a vision of God's creation on the move, from God its source towards God the goal. . . ." [13] And yet, one need not be a Christian to hold this conception of history.

Closely related to the foregoing philosophies of history, but not identical with any of them, is the spiritual interpretation. Religious belief is but one of many spiritual forces said to help shape the course of history. Among other spiritual forces said to be working to the same end are ideals, loyalty, racial pride, and notions of individual honor.[14]

GREAT MEN IN HISTORY

Interpreting the word "documents" to include all records and things which man leaves on the earth, one can readily agree with Bishop Stubbs's dictum, "No documents, no history." But it may be said with even greater truth, "no man, no documents"; for man is, after all, the subject of history and without him the only conceivable history would be the geological and the non-human biological. It is because man is central in history that historical studies are at once exciting, challenging, and perplexing. The nature of man—so open and yet so mysterious, so transparent and yet so enigmatic—must be the stuff of all philosophies of history. And in one way or another, each of these philosophies seeks an answer to the question: What makes man act the way he does? If we understood man, we would understand history; and since we do not understand him, except very imperfectly, our grasp of history remains tentative, partial, and incomplete. Anthropologist Ralph Linton observed that the planned society must await an understanding of man.[15]

As noted elsewhere in this study,* some scholars have conceived of man as essentially an economic being and history as a story of economic class-conflict. Others, as we have seen, regard him as a product of spiritual and intangible forces; and still others have interpreted him and his history in terms of physical environment. In the welter of philosophies, of which these are only a few, those thinkers probably come nearest the truth who can find no single clue to history but see it as a product of forces as complex as life itself.

Thomas Carlyle, celebrated for powers of vivid descriptive writing, saw history chiefly as the handiwork of great men. From his viewpoint, "Universal history, the history of what man has accomplished in this world, is at bottom the History of the Great Men who have worked here." These men were "the modellers, patterns, and in a wide sense creators, of whatever the general mass of men contrived to do or attain. . . ." The world's accomplishments "are the outer material results, the practical realisation and embodiment, of Thoughts that dwelt in the Great Men sent into the world," and the history of these men constitutes "the soul of the whole world's history. . . ." Even so, Carlyle did not see great men as perfect men or as necessarily strong men, and he recognized gradations of greatness. Thus, Rousseau was "not what I would call a strong man," and Napoleon was not as great as Cromwell.[16] To Carlyle, the hero "lives in the inward sphere of things, in the True, Divine, and Eternal," [17] and in heroes he saw the only hope for

* See below, pp. 24-25.

the troubled world of the second quarter of the nineteenth century.[18] Although the theory of human greatness was not original with Carlyle and there were ancient sources for it,[19] the Scotch historian greatly underestimated the importance of his published lectures on the subject when he wrote that "No Book of mine ever looked more insignificant to me." [20] Whether for good or ill, the work has had an enduring influence on historiography.

Like some other interpretations of history, the great-man theory seems plausible enough—up to a point. For instance, it is difficult to conceive of seventeenth-century England without a Cromwell, or early nineteenth-century Europe without a Napoleon. And yet this view is owing in no small part to the fact that these men did live and that they cut a wide swath though the history of their times. We do not know what would have happened had they never lived, and we do not know that other men might not have carved even larger niches for themselves than did these two. But we do know that neither man could have achieved what he did without the aid of countless lesser men, most of whom have gone unnoticed in history. Count Tolstoy had some understandable bias against Napoleon, since the Corsican had invaded Russia; nevertheless, one cannot but have doubts about Napoleon's "greatness" after reading the Russian novelist's analysis of the "Little Corporal," an analysis that concludes that Napoleon was but a creature of events, not their originator, and that the word "great" could not appropriately be applied to him.[21]

"Greatness" is, of course, a word subject to various interpretations and is perhaps one of the most abused words in our language. Jacob Christophe Burckhardt suggested that in trying to understand greatness, we might begin by recognizing that it "is all that we are *not*." Burckhardt was also of opinion that "not every age finds its great man, and not every great endowment finds its time." [22] As Edwin R. A. Seligman put it, "the great man influences society only when society is ready for him." If society is not ready for him, then the great man is regarded in his time as "a visionary or a failure." [23] If this is true, greatness in men becomes recognizable only when the men and the times meet, as presumably they did in the England of William Pitt, and later, of Sir Winston Churchill, and in the America of George Washington. "In 1929," says Sidney Hook, "Roosevelt would have been as helpless as Hoover; in 1933 he had his opportunity." [24]

ECONOMIC AND PHYSICAL-ENVIRONMENTAL
INFLUENCES IN HISTORY

In the labyrinth of semantics which the historian must traverse to find an understanding of what historians, philosophers, and others have said about history, he is in constant danger of becoming entangled in ambiguities and contradictions. Thus, one writer may speak of an economic interpretation of history as if this were synonymous with economic determinism, while another scholar may give to the latter term a meaning much more sweeping than is usually conveyed by the words, "economic interpretation of history." Even Charles A. Beard, whose name is associated more closely than that of any other American historian with an economic interpretation of American history, has been charged with confusing the two concepts.[25]

At the turn of the century, Edwin R. A. Seligman, Columbia University economist, published a work resulting from a comprehensive investigation of the role of economic forces in life and history. But while he saw the economic factor operative in law, politics, ethics, and morals, Seligman was an economic interpretationist, not an economic determinist. "No monistic interpretation of humanity," said he, "is possible. . . ." To the Columbia scholar, an economic interpretation of history did not mean a belief "that all history is to be explained in economic terms alone, but that the chief considerations in human progress are the social considerations, and that the important factor in social change is the economic factor." It means "not that the economic relations exert an exclusive influence, but that they exert a preponderant influence in shaping the progress of society."[26] With this latter judgment, Henri Sée was in agreement.[27]

Although the economic influence in life and thus in history is so obvious that it is accepted as a commonplace, it is not universally accepted as the determining influence. Man, "as far back as we have knowledge of him," says Sir Frederick M. Powicke, "has always refused to regard this motive as the clue to his way of life."[28] The doctrine that history is a story of class struggle and that the non-material side of life—religion, politics, law, morality, metaphysics, and ideologies—is determined by the material side, is associated with the names of Karl Marx and Friedrich Engels, especially the former. Economic determinism of the Marxian brand is thus something more than an economic interpretation of history: to the economic determinist, economic forces are not merely one of several influences in history, or even the "preponderant" influence, as Seligman and Sée believed, but the determining or conditioning influence.[29]

While it is doubtful that any significant percentage of American historians are economic determinists, many of them may subscribe, with varying degrees and shades of meaning, to the economic interpretation of history as developed by Seligman. Carl Becker, who accepted much of the class-conflict theory of the past, but who rejected the communist prediction of the future, was convinced that Americans must choose between Socialism, Social Democracy, Communism, and Fascism. Becker's personal choice was Social Democracy, an extension of the welfare-state philosophy of the "New Deal" of the 1930's.[30] And Charles A. Beard stated in 1933 that he believed the world was moving toward a "collectivist democracy."[31]

Beard's writings on American history, especially his studies of the formation and adoption of the Constitution of 1787, and of Jeffersonian Democracy, did much to give an economic bias to a generation of American historians.[32] The result has been a long and continuing debate among historians as to the nature and soundness of the Beard thesis, and no end to the controversy is in sight. To the extent that the debate causes students to probe more deeply into the meaning of history, it may be conjectured that the effect of Beard's interpretation is precisely what its author would have desired. And the influence has not been limited to American historians. Thus, Norwegian historian Halvdan Koht wrote in 1930 that one of the conditions back of the formation of the American constitutional union in 1787 "was the necessity felt by the upper classes of uniting defensively against the revolutionary risings of the lower classes."[33] In support of this view, however, Koht could have cited evidence reaching far back of Beard's time, especially to the correspondence of George Washington.

Closely related to the economic interpretation of history are the geographical and physical-environmental interpretations. English historian Henry Thomas Buckle emphasized these influences in his study of civilization, chiefly the English and Scottish.[34] In America, a pioneer work was Ellen Churchill Semple's *American History and Its Geographic Conditions,* a study that did not make the mistake of dissociating geographic from human factors. Thus, in the American "advance from ocean to ocean geographic conditions . . . became factors so strong that just for the sturdy energy of the Anglo-Saxon race they became determinants." "A less vigorous people," she added, "would hardly have responded to the educative influences of this peculiar environment." [35] The frontier thesis of Frederick Jackson Turner that leading American intellectual traits are traceable to the frontier influence had in it strong overtones of economics, geography, and sociology.[36] Insofar as the thesis emphasized the role of free land in shaping American social development, it owed much to Italian economist Achille Loria, who had made the same point in a more general way, and whose researches were acknowledged by Turner.[37] Like the Beard thesis, the Turner interpretation of American history has had a large and devoted following, and on it, too, debate as to its merits seems endless.

HISTORY AS LITERATURE

But history has also been conceived of as literature, and Herodotus of Halicarnassus has been called the "father of history," primarily of literary history. As literature, Herodotus's history makes fascinating reading. Lord Macaulay, while paying tribute to the beauty of Herodotus's language and style, noted nevertheless that the "father of history" wrote much in the vein of servants' gossip.[38] His history, dealing with the Graeco-Persian Wars, was divided into nine books, the first named for Clio, the Muse of history, the others for her eight sisters. If he often wrote from hearsay, as Macaulay observes, Herodotus made no effort to conceal this fact. Indeed, he begins his narrative with the equivocal statement: "According to the Persians best qualified in history, the Phoenicians began the quarrel." Had Herodotus inserted a footnote for this statement and listed several historians and their works in support of it, his method would have seemed strikingly modern. Shortly after this initial statement, Herodotus twice used the phrase, "they say," followed by other qualifying phraseology, such as "according to the Persian story," and "as report says." [39]

In modern times, the history-as-literature point of view has been represented with much distinction by the Macaulay- Trevelyan family, most recently by the late George Macaulay Trevelyan, noted historian of England, whose works exemplify the best, both as literature and as history. Trevelyan disclaims any philosophy of history, holding that philosophy is something one brings to history rather than something one extracts from it. And yet, as previously noted, if one's conception of the purposes of history is a philosophy, then certainly Trevelyan had a philosophy of history. It was his view, for instance, that history should instruct and inspire, an end that could be reached only by selecting, organizing, and presenting history according to some preconceived pattern.

If the concept of history as a science had its leading representative in Germany, it was there also that the *Methodenstreit,* or conflict over whether history was a science or an art, developed.[40] The necessity of getting at the facts, as the first duty of a historian, caused some scholars to take an extremely critical attitude toward history as literature. John B. Bury said that the historian was no more obliged to tell his story artistically than the astronomer was to dress up his account of the stars in literary garb. History, said Bury, might provide material for literature, but was itself a science.[41] Writing over a half-century after Bury's statement was made, Herbert Butterfield, professor of modern history at Cambridge, maintained that the historian was not obliged to be a mere transcriber of information "with colourless, passionless impartiality." And Clio, said he, was not to be trusted as an infallible guide, but must be regarded as "an old reprobate" given to cheating and trickery.[42]

America has not been without historians whose writings were celebrated both as literature and as history. Among earlier historians, Francis Parkman and Henry Adams were outstanding for works of this character, and among later ones, Carl Becker was probably without a peer. It has been observed of Parkman that, in matters of style, he was influenced more by Cooper, Irving, and Scott than by historians, and that he had the valuable knack of being able to read historians for their facts without absorbing their bad style.[43] Carl Becker, noting John Spencer Bassett's temptation to classify Parkman with modern "scientific" historians, because of Parkman's use of sources, rather than with the earlier literary historians, remarks that had Parkman "only written badly, no one could question his scientific standing." [44] Becker himself was described in 1935 by J. Franklin Jameson as "the most brilliant historical writer that we have in this country." [45]

To say that we have had but few historians whose works were distinguished literature is not to say that all other historians have written badly. On the contrary, there are scores of historians who write well, and there are relatively few that do not observe at least the elementary canons of correct writing. But accurate, correct writing can be very dull writing and in itself will win no literary accolades. It is the historian who is able to exceed the requirements of correct writing—who is able to find the elegant or striking, and at the same time accurate, word or phrase which lifts his discourse out of the commonplace—whose work presumably will be read as literature as well as history. However deficient he may have been as a scholar, amateur historian Theodore Roosevelt was on strong ground when he argued in his presidential address before the American Historical Association that histories in order to be of great and lasting influence must be readable. "Many learned people," said Roosevelt, "seem to feel that the quality of readableness in a book is one which warrants suspicion." [46]

As to this, historians probably would say that whether "readableness" in a book warrants suspicion would depend upon how this quality is achieved; for scholars are fearful that a conscious effort to be "interesting" may lead to compromising with facts to achieve that end. Although Jules Michelet said that history is *une résurrection*,[47] and Johan Huizinga has stressed the importance in historianship of imagination and ability to recreate the past so that voices long silent may be heard again,[48] these, obviously, are qualities to be used with caution. As Herbert Butterfield warns, efforts to write "resurrection history" may cause the historian to include in his narrative something more than actual history.[49]

THE UNIVERSAL APPROACH IN HISTORY

In the Western world, one of the earliest proponents of universal history was Voltaire. The universal approach was also employed by Georg Wilhelm Friedrich Hegel, one of the most powerful influences in modern historiography. More distinguished as a philosopher than as a historian, Hegel, despite his broad view of history, was much interested in the national state, especially Prussia. The latter he saw as the fulfillment of the individual's desire for liberty, a boon which he said found its best expression in organized society and under limitations.[50] Karl Lamphrecht, likewise more concerned with the general than with the particular, saw society, not the individual, as the proper unit of historical study. This view placed him in sharp contrast to Leopold von Ranke and the "scientific" historians and caused some critics to declare him a social-psychologist.[51]

And as we have seen, English historian Henry Thomas Buckle adopted the civilization approach. His own writing was confined chiefly to the history of English and Scottish civilization, not because he lacked appreciation for the remainder of civilization, but because he felt a single lifetime insufficient to investigate all civilization. Contemptuous of history as it had been written, because he believed it dealt with unimportant facts only, Buckle said that it left the student of civilization in a position where he must quarry for facts as though there had been no previous writing on the subject. For facts supplied by historians "neither furnish new truths, nor . . . supply the means by which new truths may be discovered."[52]

In the twentieth century, the grand sweep of civilization has come under the scrutiny of several scholars, notably Oswald Spengler and Arnold Toynbee. Believing that history has laws and is predictable, Spengler concluded that the West had passed its cultural peak and was in decline, while the more optimistic Toynbee, agreeing with the first part of Spengler's thesis, sees a chance for the survival of the West, provided it accepts religious and moral discipline.[53]

But civilization is more than Western civilization, and many years ago, Immanuel Kant (1724–1804) conceived the tendency of history as being toward a "universal cosmopolitan condition" in which the highest capacities of the human race would have an opportunity to develop.[54] William H. McNeill, professor of history at the University of Chicago, likewise foresees an eventual "cosmopolitan world society" which, because of the influence of Western science and technology in bringing it about, will "bear a Western imprint." [55]

Thus, although most historians have eschewed general or world history as too large for research purposes, and are skeptical of attempts at world syntheses, the universal approach has not lacked distinguished representatives among both historians and philosophers. Jacques Pirenne, in the first volume of a projected general history, says that only through comparative studies of civilization can conclusions of a scientific, sociological, and moral nature be reached.[56] And, as we have seen, Karl Jaspers, after surveying the problem of historical philosophy from the universal standpoint, evolved a "schema of total conception." Perhaps historians Thomas Carlyle and James Schouler (1839–1920) were typical exponents of generalist and particularist points of view. Carlyle suggested that most historians are "Artisans" who fail to see the bearing of their specialties on the larger pattern of history, whereas the "Artists" never fail to see the relation of the particular to the general.[57] But Schouler, in a paper read before the American Historical Association in 1889, said: "In the present age one must be ignorant of much if he would be proficient in something." [58]

III

HISTORICISM, RELATIVISM, AND OTHER CONCEPTS

UNTIL RECENTLY, at least, it has been the good fortune of the historian that his craft has been unencumbered by a system of specialized semantics. In the main, he has been able to express himself in language understandable to any intelligent adult reader, and he has also been able to present much of history's findings in terms that school youths can understand. But during our generation, conditions affecting historianship have greatly changed. It is now appreciated better than ever before that history impinges on disciplines that do employ specialized semantics. And in an effort to utilize and present accurately the contributions of these related subjects, the historian finds himself using words and phrases hitherto peculiar to economics, philosophy, psychology, or sociology. Often these words have no fixed meanings; and in economics, specialization has gone so far that communication even between specialists has become difficult.

HISTORICISM

One of the words that perplex the historian is "historicism"—a word defined by historians, philosophers, and behavioral scientists in so many and contradictory ways as to leave the reader with the impression that it can have no clear-cut meaning. And yet it is an unavoidable word: it looms large in countless books and articles treating of historical method and philosophy, particularly in discussions of the question whether history is a science or not, whether it is objective, whether it has laws, or whether it is the "truth." Webster's latest unabridged dictionary defines the word as being both a theory of history and a practice of writing history according to the theory. In the Webster definition are implied such concepts as historical determinism, relativism, objectivity, history-mindedness, and laws of change. It is thus not surprising that, because of the varied meanings attached to it, the word has been equated with philosophy of history. According to this view, one's concept of history is historicism and the holder of the concept is a historicist.[1] But while this may suffice as an overall definition, it will give little assistance to the reader struggling with a book that uses the word in some restricted way.

For this reason, it seems that every writer who uses the word should make clear at the outset what he means by it. Karl R. Popper writes of "theistic historicism," "naturalistic historicism," "spiritual historicism," and "economic historicism" to indicate different interpretations of history and thus suggests that there is no one way of looking at history that represents the totality of meaning embodied in the word. Yet Popper defines "the central historicist doctrine" as "the doctrine that history is controlled by specific historical or evolutionary laws whose discovery would enable us to prophesy the destiny of man." [2] This he regards as "sheer superstition," although he does not reject social prediction in its entirety.[3] On occasion, Charles A. Beard used historicism as though it meant the Rankean type of historiography.[4] And Crane Brinton uses the term as meaning a study of the past in order to understand the present and predict the future.[5]

The dilemma that confronts the student seeking a concise and generally acceptable definition of historicism was ably shown by Dwight E. Lee and Robert N. Beck in a brief analysis of the problem in 1954. But the definition with which these scholars concluded their survey, in rejecting not only "relationism" and "relativism" but also Popper's concept of historical prediction, poses problems. For while Lee's and Beck's definition agrees with a part of the New Webster's definition, it completely disagrees with one of its variant definitions, and does not include "the practice of writing or treating history" at all.[6]

For the foregoing reasons, one can sympathize with the attitude implicit in a recent discussion of historicism under the heading,

"Every Historian His Own Historicist." [7] For the conclusion seems inescapable that there is no single definition of the word that has gained general acceptance among historians or other scholars, and that readers must hope, therefore, that writers using the term will explain what they mean by it. However unsatisfactory it may seem to some students, philosopher Morton White's definition of historicism as "the attempt to explain facts by reference to earlier facts," has at least the dual merit of brevity and lucidity.[8] If a writer using the word does not define it, perhaps it will not be unreasonable for the reader to assume that the discussion of it will be ambiguous and that only confusion, not enlightenment, can come of it.

RELATIVISM

The Ranke ideal of an objective history that would tell precisely how things had happened, was, as noted, made the governing principle of American historiography during the latter part of the nineteenth century. This early aim of the American historical profession to write history in accordance with canons of German scholarship was acclaimed in 1935 by Professor Theodore C. Smith as "a noble dream." [9] The phrase, "that noble dream," was used by Charles A. Beard in an answering article,[10] with the result that a widely used guide to the study and reading of American history says Beard dismissed the objectivity ideal as "that noble dream." [11] Far from regarding the Ranke ideal as in any sense "noble," Beard thought it unrealistic and tinged with hypocrisy.

While Beard yielded to none in the matter of scientific method in history, he insisted that the selection and arrangement of facts in written history were inevitably subjective. Perhaps but few historians would take a contrary position. Thus, Max Farrand wrote in 1918 of one of his histories: "As is the case with every historical study . . . the personal element of selection and emphasis has been the controlling factor." [12] Even Samuel Eliot Morison, one of Beard's severest critics, while insisting that he stands "firm" on the famous Ranke dictum, concedes that "complete 'scientific' objectivity is unattainable by the historian" and that the latter's procedures "must be governed by his philosophy of life." Morison asserts, moreover, that historians "from Ranke down" would not have "denied that their philosophy of life influenced, if it did not dictate, their selection, emphasis, and arrangement."

Of course, there is wide agreement among Rankeans and non-Rankeans. If the former group admits subjectivity in the quest for truth, the latter stoutly insists that, despite its subjectivity, its quest is also for the truth.

And if, as Professor Morison suggests, complete objectivity is unattainable by the historian, it may be that complete consistency in attitude toward problems of historical interpretation, even by craftsmen of the greatest skill, is likewise unattainable. Thus in 1922 when Arthur M. Schlesinger published his *New Viewpoints in American History,* he said that he could not hope to have completely succeeded "in eliminating the personal equation." "Every teacher of history," he said, "evolves a philosophy of history which will find expression in spite of all efforts at repression. . . ." [14] Yet, in 1962, when he conducted a rating of American presidents by a panel composed principally of professional historians and a reader charged that these were influenced by their political convictions, Professor Schlesinger replied "that the training of a competent historian should enable him to rise above his political feelings in forming judgments" and that he felt the members "did take objective viewpoints." [15]

But regardless of the school to which he belongs, the historian must know that, even after he has exhausted his best efforts to discover the full truth, he has succeeded only partially. For history, as the late James Westfall Thompson once said, "is as a window thrown open to the night—we see lights and hear voices, but that is all." [16]

Since the complete truth of history lies beyond human grasp, and only bits and pieces of history selected in accordance with the historian's "presentism" or other philosophy, is possible, it may be asked where this leaves the doctrines of fixed truth and morals. It leaves them un-fixed, as concepts whose meaning is not absolute, but relative to the particular age in which they appear, and to the economic, political, or other prepossessions of the historian. Thus, Henry Charles Lea, differing from Lord Acton, asserted in 1904 that there are no fixed moral values in history. Lea believed in "the temporary and variable character of morals," rather than in "a universal and inflexible standard" in this realm. The country, the times, and the people were the determinants.[17] Philosophers John Dewey, Karl R. Popper, and Alfred North Whitehead have taken similar positions.[18]

To some persons, relativism is a vastly disturbing philosophy, and the charge has even been made that it will, if followed, return humanity to "skepticism, nihilism, irrationalism, and finally . . . to barbarism." [19] Obviously, relativism reaches beyond historianship. Empiricism, or pragmatism, holds that there are no absolutes and that everything must be tested and evaluated by its workability; relativism in history is closely akin to these views. Charles A. Beard noted, however, that relativism, being itself a concept of history, is relative to the time of its birth and usage, and may be expected to pass with time. From Beard's viewpoint, since the whole truth is unknowable, the historian's efforts to get at the truth must be characterized as "an act of faith." [20]

As the foregoing discussion suggests, differences in attitudes toward relativism may derive from differences in overall philosophies of the scholars holding them, and thus be irreconcilable.[21] Historians' criticism of relativism usually has been that it leads to slipshod methods in research and to a maximum of subjectivity and propaganda for causes. The criticism by historian James C. Malin, however, goes beyond this. In a chapter entitled "Adventures into the Unknown: Relativist 'Man-Afraid-of-His-Mind,' " Malin accuses relativists of being afraid to explore the unknown and to reach beyond space and time in quest of the "Absolute" or the "One." In a word, Malin seems to be issuing a call for historians to become "metahistorians" and attempt to break through the boundaries of documentable facts and enter the realm of mysticism.[22]

In his metahistorianship, Malin has distinguished company. Arnold J. Toynbee, although he tries in his writing to combine vision with empiricism, admits to being a trans-rationalist and a metahistorian, and frankly testifies to several experiences of a visionary or revelatory kind.[23] Gentle and humane in his outlook, Toynbee certainly is far removed in his thinking from Friedrich Nietzsche, the apostle of selfishness; nevertheless, there is a striking similarity in the intuitive experiences of the two men. Nietzsche said that the basic idea of his work came to him on an August day in 1881 while he was walking in the woods by a lake.[24] And

Toynbee tells us how, while he was walking in London shortly after World War I, he "found himself in communion" with all history, past, present, and future, and "was directly aware" of the flow of history through him, and of "his own life welling like a wave in the flow of this vast tide." [25]

But metahistorianship to one side, some persons, with perhaps too much emphasis upon the semantic similarity of the two words, have thought of philosophical *relativism* as being the counterpart of Einstein's theory of *relativity* in physics.[26] Actually, of course, if one is thinking in terms of constants to which other things are relative, the concept goes far back of Einstein's time. Thinking in the physical and philosophical realms are not necessarily complementary, however, and, altogether, it would appear the part of wisdom to approach with the greatest caution any supposed analogous relationship of historical or philosophical relativism with the Einstein theory of relativity.

PRESENTISM

That history should aim to explain the present is a widely accepted idea. Its popularity springs partly from the dilemma in which the historian finds himself if he rejects the presentist view; for if he believes that history does not help explain the present, then presumably he believes that a study of the past has a value largely for its own sake and for purposes of mental discipline. Some scholars believe that such a viewpoint would reduce history to the level of obscurantist antiquarianism. Nevertheless, the idea has been ably represented by Michael Oakeshott, professor of political science at the London School of Economics. As he sees it, the historian's concern must be the past as such, and the past's detachment, immobility, deadness, and irrelevance "are not defects to be removed, but blessed virtue to be enjoyed." [27] A contrary view is held by philosopher R. G. Collingwood, who insists that the past in itself is nothing and has significance only to the extent that it explains the present. The historian's goal, says he, "is knowledge of the present" and "round that everything must revolve." [28] And Pieter Geyl, professor of history at the University of Utrecht, regards history not as "an inventory of dead people and dead things, but a key to life. . . ." [29] As for all this, the late Edward P. Cheyney warned that history should do more than help men understand the present; for the present is no sooner arrived than it is gone. History, he said, should chart the future; and to this end, he announced, as we have seen, his conception of historical laws.[30]

While it is commonly said that the successful historian must have the imagination to re-live the period of which he writes, it is also generally recognized that he cannot avoid being influenced by the spirit of his own time (*Zeitgeist*).[31] Benedetto Croce has said that "History is contemporary thought about the past," [32] and Jacob Burckhardt has said that it "is the record of what one age finds worthy of note in another." [33] Some presentist students have advocated that history be studied backwards—that instead of beginning with early times and moving forward, one should begin with the present and move backward. This notion, says Oakeshott, is the "practical" or rational view of the world, but it cannot be the view of the historian.[34]

Professor J. H. Hexter has shown in a recent study that present-minded and history-minded scholars have much in common and that all historians are present-minded in that they write in terms of their own times and in the light of contemporary findings in their specialties. But he warns that extreme present-mindedness can lead the historian into vain efforts to relate everything in the past to the present and try to make it contribute something to contemporary society. This, he avers, makes the historian into a "do-gooder." [35] But presentism and criticism thereof are by no means recent developments. Ibn Khaldûn called attention to the danger of interpreting the past in terms of the present. Because "of ignorance of changes in the environment within which history unfolds," the historian "falls into an abyss of error" when he measures the past by his own observations." "The fact of change," said he, is "a hidden pitfall in historiography" and" a sore affliction . . . deeply hidden." [36]

The theory of presentism has perhaps never received a more succinct statement than that made in 1925 by James Harvey Robinson in the Preface to his *An Introduction to the History of Western Europe*. Observing that when the first edition of the work was published in 1902 it was believed that Europe was stabilized, and that since then unexpected developments had occurred, Robinson explained that he had rewritten and expanded the treatment of events since 1815. To Robinson, history ought to be rewritten from the vantage point of the present, and only those facts be extracted from the past as would serve to explain the present. "It is the prime function of history," he said, "to substantiate and illustrate the inexorable dependence of the present on what has gone before." Moreover, the historian who believes that history should prepare readers for intelligent citizenship by improving their understanding of the present, "will inevitably make his selection of material with this end in view." [37]

It seems clear that if he accepts Robinson's viewpoint, the historian will not begin with the past and work forward, but will begin with the present and work backward; and yet, Robinson's history was not written in this way. It seems, therefore, that Robinson meant only that in dealing with the past the historian should constantly be thinking of the present and weighing and evaluating all included facts of the past in terms of our own day. Robinson's presentism also received expression in the history of modern Europe written in collaboration with Charles A. Beard. The writers acknowledged that they had "constantly subordinated the past to the present," yet felt that they had dealt no "less fairly" with earlier times "than they would have done had they merely narrated the events with no ulterior object." [38]

It may be said with some assurance that presentism, in the sense that it connotes a belief that a study of the past should illumine the present, has been one of the most generally accepted principles of the American historical profession. In the early years of American historianship as an organized profession, the idea of presentism, although the word itself was not used, was frequently advanced. A study of American Historical Association presidential addresses has shown, according to Herman Ausubel, that presentism was a commonly held view by the Association's annually elected leaders, and that the broad approach to history was appreciated long before Robinson popularized the idea.[39] Moreover, the Association's "Committee of Seven" appointed in the 1890's to make a study of history in the schools stated the principle in strong terms. Six of the Committee members were college or university professors of history and were of the highest professional reputation: Andrew C. McLaughlin, Chairman (Michigan), Herbert B. Adams (Johns Hopkins), Albert Bushnell Hart (Harvard), Charles H. Haskins (Wisconsin), Lucy M. Salmon (Vassar), and H. Morse Stephens

(Cornell). In their report made in 1898, the Committee said they wished "to emphasize the thought that appreciation and sympathy for the present is best assured by a study of the past. . . ." The presentist idea also found indirect expression in the Committee's view that history contributed "directly" to "good and useful citizenship," and in certain other items of their report.[40] A report by an Association "Committee of Five," made a dozen years later, observed that history and government, "if properly taught," should aid in giving students "an appreciation of the present and a sense of social life and social responsibility. . . ." [41]

The principle was also stated a little later by Charles M. Andrews, in a paper on the place of modern European history in the college curriculum. Said Andrews: ". . . in the highest sense of our science we study the past that we may better understand the present. . . ." [42] And the highly regarded Channing and Hart (later, Channing, Hart, and Turner) *Guide to the Study and Reading of American History* likewise gave presentism a boost. The "principal purpose" of historical study is "to put the student into such a frame of mind that he may apply known principles to things with which he is for the first time confronted." [43] Frederick J. Turner said that "one of the most important functions of the historian is to enable the present age to understand itself by understanding its origin and growth." [44]

In England, the question of history's relation to the present was represented by the "Bury-Trevelyan controversy," Cambridge professor, John B. Bury, insisting upon the strictly scientific character of history, and Professor George M. Trevelyan, of the same university, arguing for an interpretative as well as a factual history. Regarding the entire discussion, both in the United States and abroad, W. H. Walsh, professor of logic and metaphysics at Edinburgh University, says that major historians "have not hesitated to put the facts into perspective as well as to seek them out, and in so doing have contrived to carry out what Trevelyan rightly saw to be a major task of history, the making men aware of the character of their own time by seeing it in comparison and by contrast with another." [45] If this attitude is, as Michael Oakeshott suggests, what the "world" expects of the historian, there would seem to be strong evidence in the writings of American historians that, on this issue in the United States, the "world" is winning.

CAUSALITY

It probably would astound the average reader of history to be told that there is a serious division of opinion among competent historians whether historianship should concern itself with causation, or, indeed, whether causation is a word that can even properly be applied to written history. It may be supposed that the role of cause and effect in history is taken for granted by most persons who take the time to read history, and it is the assumed interplay of these factors which goes far toward explaining whatever popularity history enjoys. To say that causes of events are unascertainable would seem far-fetched to the average intelligent layman. For much of life impinges on questions of causation. As Raymond Aron observes, the judge tries to answer the question, "Whose fault is it?" And this means that the judge must reach conclusions as to causes of events in litigation.[46] Friedrich Meinecke said that men wish to find guidance and wisdom in history and that it is this wish which attracts them to the subject. But if there is no fairly clear connection between cause and effect in history, it may well be questioned whether the subject can afford the reader either wisdom or any worthwhile guidance.[47]

Charles A. Beard, one of the most widely acclaimed historians, insisted that the words "cause" and "causality" should not be used in written history at all.[48] That Beard could hold this view without damaging his reputation with the reading public, may be attributed to two circumstances: first, the view was usually not explicit in Beard's major writings, and, second, it was never consistently held by him. On the purely philosophical side, long before Beard's time, the skeptic David Hume doubted that it could be demonstrated that every object owes its existence to a cause;[49] however, this sophisticated view has not greatly influenced historical writing. Commenting on the physical world, J. S. Mill noted the difficulties encountered in trying to assign a cause for any event, since every cause must itself be caused.[50] As to this, perhaps Benedetto Croce is correct in saying that *first* causes can never be found; and perhaps Patrick Gardiner is also correct in saying that there are no "Real Causes." Instead of causes we have explanations and interpretations of history by scholars operating on different levels and in different contexts. The "search for causes and origins," says Geoffrey

Barraclough, professor of modern history in the University of Liverpool, "only brings us up against the ultimate mysteries." [51]

French medievalist Marc Bloc noted that the idea of causation was one with which both scientists and historians must deal, and that misunderstanding of the present results from misunderstanding the past. Nevertheless, Bloc realized that relationships between cause and effect were not always clearly established. Using the Black Death and its consequences as an illustrative problem, Bloc observed that if the Black Death virus was the main cause of Europe's depopulation, the rapid spread of the disease was owing to certain social and mental conditions of the times.[52]

Dissent from the negative viewpoint on causality has been widespread. For instance, Henry Thomas Buckle, like Edward Hallett Carr a century later, believed that causes in history were ascertainable, and, for certain great events—the French Revolution, as an example—he illustrated his thesis.[53] Moreover, University of California historian, Frederick J. Teggart, seeking a clue to institutions, said that in history "it becomes evident that everywhere the beginnings of political organization have been determined by the physical disposition of the land." [54] As we have seen, Italian economist Achille Loria likewise emphasized the effect of free land upon social development, and Loria's thought influenced Frederick J. Turner when he formulated his frontier thesis that free land was an important factor in determining the course of American history.[55] Another American historian of the frontier, Walter Prescott Webb, noting that the Great Plains blocked Southern expansion, suggests strongly that this factor contributed signally to the South's losing the Civil War.[56]

In a more general way than that expounded by Loria, Turner, and Webb, economist Edwin R. A. Seligman regarded economic forces as the "preponderant" influence in history, including the shaping of moral and social conceptions.[57] What all of these writers are saying is that physical and economic conditions are *causes* in history and that they have effects on the political, social, and economic development of society. And if it is the business of the historian, as Richard B. Schlatter says it is, "to describe the actions of a portion of humanity living at a specified time and place and to explain why it behaved in certain ways," [58] then the view seems inescapable that the historian must be concerned with causation.

He needs to know both the why and the what of history; however, as it has wisely been said, when he asks for the why as well as the what, history responds by giving him some more of the what.

To believe in the reciprocal action of cause and effect does not mean necessarily that one believes in *laws* of history. Of course, if one can accept the belief in historical laws, one not only accepts causation but also has an easy answer to the question of why things happen when and in the way they do. Still, one may believe in the principle of cause and effect—that every effect has one or more causes and vice versa—without believing that the totality of causes and effects comprises one or more historical laws. He may believe that the number of instances of cause and effect in history is infinite and that no ordering, no classifying, no categorizing of these instances is possible. Or he may believe, with philosopher Nathan Rotenstreich, of the Hebrew University, Jerusalem, that while the past is the cause of the present, one cannot carry the assumption of causality beyond this generalization.[59] Historians who formulate laws of history or who make much of cause and effect in human developments are in some respects closer to sociology than to history. For the "father of sociology," Auguste Comte, believed that sociology's object was "to explain all historical facts. . . ." [60]

The search by the historian for causality in history is inseparably linked to his scheme of values. And schemes of values raise anew the problem of subjectivity. Heinrich Rickert recognized that values guide the historian in deciding what to investigate, but he believed that once this decision was made, the historian could proceed objectively. To Rickert, it is not the task of the historian to say whether things are valuable or not, but only to say what was. Assignment of praise or blame is beyond the limits of history, and if one has values in history, his history is not a science.[61]

Friedrich Meinecke observes that the first part of the Rickert thesis is sound, but that the second is impossible. For in the process of presenting facts, says Meinecke, value judgments are made explicitly, or they are made implicitly, as in Ranke's writings. On this last point, Meinecke and Beard are in agreement: the historian decides to study, not all the facts of the past, but only those thought by him to be "essential" or most "influential"; and selection of facts of these kinds is a subjective process. In recognizing the relationship of causality and values, Meinecke warned that "subjectivism run riot" could ruin historianship, and that protection against this tendency can be found in a recognition that causalities and values are interdependent.[62]

Thus, when one considers causes of the American Revolution, of the American Civil War, or of the Great Depression—to apply the Meinecke doctrine—one is inevitably caught up in a weighing and balancing of factors in the background of each of these movements. For instance, to one student of the American Revolution the main cause of the upheaval seems to have been economic; to another, constitutional; and to another, political. The Civil War, say some students, resulted from a constitutional cleavage between North and South; it was an effect of economic differences between the sections, say others; it was a result of slavery, say still others. The Great Depression in the United States was precipitated by world conditions, says one school of thought; it was essentially a product of faulty American domestic and foreign policies, says another. In history, *effects* are obvious; we could not miss them if we tried. Our lives are effects, and from birth till death we spend our lives in a milieu composed of an infinite number of effects. But the *causes* of these effects are usually hidden and elusive, and the historian in trying to find and isolate them is guided by a value system peculiar to his own life experiences.

Moreover, as Dr. Samuel Johnson pointed out, there is no balance as between cause and effect. "It seems to be almost the universal error of historians," said Johnson, "that every effect has a proportionate cause. . . ." On the contrary, "the operations of life, whether private or public, admit no such laws." "The caprices of voluntary agents," said the Doctor, "laugh at calculation." Further: "It is not always that there is a strong reason for a great event." [63] More recently, Edinburgh University historian Richard Pares noted that while "history is especially a study of causality," any *system* in history is precluded by certain variables, which he identified as climate, war, religion, technology and science, and conditions of production.[64]

THE UNKNOWABLE IN HISTORY

The search for causation in history is all the more frustrating because so much of the past must remain unknown. For if history consists of all that man has said, thought, or done since he first appeared on the earth, it seems clear that recorded or written history can be only a fragment of the total. Many of man's physical deeds left no identifying marks for the historian, and the great bulk of his words, even those spoken by persons of timeless intellectual interest, went unrecorded and are irretrievable. The thoughts of men are even more elusive than their words and deeds, and excepting the clues afforded him by what men have said or done, the historian is much in the dark as he enters the realm of intellectual history.

But the more elusive the facts of history are, the keener becomes the historian's curiosity about them. We know from records much of what Socrates said and did, but we would like to know the extent to which his words and deeds reflected his thoughts. And we have a similar curiosity about other important personages, from Alexander and Caesar to Cromwell, Pitt, Washington, Napoleon, Lincoln, and Wilson. Did these men reveal to anyone their full reasons for actions on matters of great moment, such, for example, as Lincoln's decision on Fort Sumter and the Emancipation Proclamation, and Wilson's decision on entering World War I and on rejecting League of Nations reservations? It will be recognized, of course, that historical personages, like lesser men, may not always have known precisely what made them act as they did, and it is at this point that the psychology of the subconscious may offer more clues for the historian than any amount of formal research in the records.

Count von Bismarck once observed that the history of international relations was not to be found in official diplomatic reports—that it was in the private correspondence and the confidential verbal communications of the moving personages that the true story of these affairs was to be found.[65] Granting the wisdom of this observation, may we not at the same time hypothesize that even the total of official and private documents will never give us the full story? For it is difficult to escape a feeling that there is a residue of unknowable truth represented by the principal actors' private thoughts which never find expression in either spoken or written words.

The impossibility of ever knowing all the thoughts, words, and deeds of the human past caused Carl Becker to conclude that there

are two histories, one, "the actual series of events that once occurred," the other, "the ideal series that we affirm and hold in
memory." For this reason, Becker identified history "with knowledge of history," and held that "much the greater part" of the
events which constitute history "in some ultimate sense" we could
not know, "not even that they occurred. . . ." [66] This view of the
duality of history has been sharply challenged on the ground that
the only history is necessarily the known history, and that to speak
of an unknown history is a contradiction in terms.[67] That is, we
know recorded history, and while we may imagine or suspect that
this is not the whole of history, we really do not know that it is not.
But Becker qualified his statement by saying that "for all practical
purposes," history is the known history, and his concept of a second
or an unknown history seems to have been an hypothesis based
upon what is known of man and his habits. We know, for instance,
that men do not reveal all that they think or know, and we are
aware that certain historical personages have succeeded by various
ways in covering up their tracks. Assuming that men through the
ages have conducted themselves in these matters in much the same
way, we arrive at the hypothesis that there must be a large segment
of history that is unknown and unknowable. If this is the correct
reading of Becker, then he is probably much nearer than his critic
to the thinking of the generality of historians.[68]

HISTORY AS THOUGHT AND AS AN ACT OF FAITH

In a powerful and incisive analysis of the meaning of history,
Charles A. Beard in 1933 categorized history as past actuality, as
record, and as thought. History as past actuality he regarded as
one of three things: a chaos, a cycle, or a straight-line or spiraling
movement. Agreeing with Benedetto Croce's statement that history
is contemporary thought about the past, Beard maintained that
history could be nothing more than facts selected, arranged, and
interpreted within a frame of reference conceived by the historian.
And since selection, arrangement, and interpretation are processes
of thought, Beard concluded that written history is essentially
thought.

But one may ask, Is not history, including that written by Professor Beard, potentially something more than thought? If written

history is history at all, as Beard readily acknowledged it to be, it must contain some facts about the past. Thus, *The Rise of American Civilization,* by Professor Beard and Mary Beard, while it contains much interpretation or thought, also contains a multitude of generally accepted facts of American history. True enough, the selection, arrangement, and interpretation of these facts by the Beards constituted an intellectual process; and certainly had they chosen to do so, the authors might have included some facts they omitted and might have omitted some which they included. Moreover, the whole scheme of their emphasis and interpretation (frame of reference) could have been altered had they wished to do so. While their book may represent merely what the Beards thought about the past of American civilization, its facts might be used by another historian to construct quite a different synthesis. For despite all the care the historian may devote to their selection, arrangement, and emphasis, facts have a way of transcending an author's frame of reference. And while an author may flatter himself that the intellectual processes required by his frame of reference actually constitute the history he has written, the reader may regard more highly the facts adduced by the author than what the author thinks about them. This means that each reader of a written history will form his own image of the facts he encounters, and that, potentially, there may be as many histories as there are readers of it.

But this is not to say that the theory of written history "as thought" is not essentially true. The theory's soundness will be evident to almost anyone who reads two books on the same subject. Thus, when two competent historians are able to take a given set of facts and produce two radically different interpretations, the phenomenon can be attributed to only one cause: a difference in the thinking of the two authors about the facts. To one historian, for example, the Boston Tea Party may seem to have been something altogether glorious and sublime, while to another it may seem to have been something abominable both as to ethics and law. Yet the *fact* of the Boston Tea Party is not in dispute between the two writers, nor are a host of collateral and subsidiary facts. Nevertheless, as Carl Becker has told us, each historian forms an image of the facts in accordance with his own experience.[71] And, as it has been well said, the historian may look at the past through a glass that is both translucent and reflective, and the "truth" that comes through to him may be but a reflection of his own prepossessions.[72] To Eric Kahler, history is "the indissoluble interaction between actuality and conceptuality."[73]

Preserved facts constitute history "as record," but it is not this kind of history to which the theory of "history as thought" is applied by Professor Beard. It is "written history," the kind of history found on shelves of libraries, the kind that history professors and graduate students produce, that Beard had in mind. History "as actuality" is, of course, dismissed by Beard as being beyond the human grasp. Whence, then, comes the difference between history "as record" and the "written history" which evolves from the record? The difference is supplied by the thought processes of the historian; and it is this which led Beard to conclude that written history is "thought." Moreover, since written history is necessarily incomplete and subjective, the production of it is "an act of faith." [74] This last view is not peculiar to Beard, and it has been said that in the natural sciences as well as in history, all actions based upon hypotheses are acts of faith.[75]

History "as thought" and "as an act of faith" is objective or scientific only in a methodological sense: the historian proceeds by induction, he tests his sources, and he honestly tries to get at the truth according to his lights. But the cold detachment of the chemist or the physicist he cannot have, and Carl Becker has said that this is fortunate, since it "would produce few histories, and none worthwhile. . . ." The "really detached mind," said he, "is a dead mind, lying among the facts of history like unmagnetized steel among iron-filings, no synthesis ever resulting, in one case or the other, to the end of time." [76] Professor Allen Johnson said much the same thing when he wrote that "A mind devoid of prepossessions is likely to be devoid of all mental furniture." [77]

HISTORIANSHIP, CITIZENSHIP, AND MORAL RESPONSIBILITY

IT IS GENERALLY RECOGNIZED that historical writing cannot avoid the spirit of the age in which it is produced. The Civil War, for example, had a pronounced impact, outside the South,[1] upon American nationalist thinking and in giving a distinct national flavor to American historical writing after 1865. As John L. Motley observed durng the war, the contest would determine whether the United States really had a national government able to make its authority felt throughout its territorial limits, or whether it belonged to the category of unstable governments whose judgments could successfully be challenged by powerful dissidents.[2] With this issue settled, the conception of the United States after 1865 as an "organism" reflected not only the influence of the Darwinian hypothesis but also a conception of a firmer nationalism than had ever been known before in the United States. The nation was, said some, "a moral person." [3] The waves of temporary concern, from reconstruction, muckraking, and the "New Freedom," to the "New Deal," civil rights, and the "New Frontiers," that have swept over the nation, have affected the thinking of all citizens, especially of historians whose task it is to study the national temper, past and present.

THE HISTORIAN AS CITIZEN IN WAR AND PEACE

From ancient days, historians have been among the active supporters of their countries' wars. Thucydides was a naval commander in the early phase of the Peloponnesian War and suffered exile for the part he played. Whatever objectivity the historian may think he observes in his research and writing, he usually modifies or entirely casts aside when his country goes to war. Indeed, if the preliminaries to war are long drawn-out, he is likely to take this action well before hostilities begin. If it seems that historians' conduct during wartime disproves any claim to objectivity that historianship may advance, it must be remembered that specialists in the natural sciences, where an even greater claim to intellectual objectivity has been made, likewise yield to wartime pressures. This social phenomenon is found not only in the United States but in other countries as well; each belligerent seeks to justify its course of action in terms of righteousness and the cause of humanity. And historians and other scholars, because of a complex of social and legal pressures and personal convictions, actively support the government, often by bearing arms or by engaging in some form of propaganda work.

· All this suggests strongly that pure rationality or objectivity are intellectual luxuries that cannot be made to harmonize with the harsh demands of war, since war itself is the antithesis of rationality and objectivity. Whatever indictment the cause of nationalism may deserve, it would seem that a large part of the charge must be that international strife causes men to sacrifice some of the most precious attributes of the human mind and spirit. This fact alone should be sufficient to give pause to advocates of the indefinite continuance of national states as against the possibility of world unity.

As noted elsewhere in this study, Herbert Baxter Adams of Johns Hopkins University took a pronounced jingoistic line on the eve of the Spanish-American War, and this he did, of all occasions, in the course of a Phi Beta Kappa address he was delivering.* World War I greatly aroused the emotions of most Americans, historians along with all others. Historians, however, were by no means of one mind as to the causes of the war or as to the relative merits of the contestants. Those who openly doubted the wisdom of American action in the war paid a price in social opprobrium, and, in some instances, in the form of discipline imposed by their employing institutions. Others, the "patriotic historians," wrote propaganda pamphlets for the government or otherwise promoted

* See below, pp. 52-53.

the war effort. In this group were some of the most eminent names in American historiography.

Writing a dozen years after the war, James Harvey Robinson noted how historians change their views with the passage of time and expressed the view that during the war historians had controlled their prejudices no better "than the man in the street" and that in all countries they were susceptible "to the prejudices of their particular tribe." Further: "They applauded the old battle cry. They blew trumpets and grasped halberds. They gulped down propaganda which in a later mood they realized was nauseous." [4] In Germany, anti-English feeling was as strong with Friedrich Meinecke[5] as anti-German feeling was with English, French, and American historians. In England, Lord Bryce, one of the most respected historians in the English-speaking world, helped propagate stories of "atrocities" the Germans were said to have committed in Belgium.

In America, the intellectual throes suffered by historians in adjusting to war were well typified by the experiences of Carl Becker. Dubious at first, as was President Wilson also, of the merits of the Allied cause in World War I, Becker finally supported it with enthusiasm, only to suffer profound disillusionment by the war's aftermath. James Ford Rhodes approved the early Wilsonian neutrality and did not think the cause of civilization and the cause of the Allies were identical. But like others who had at first been doubtful, Rhodes finally supported whole-heartedly America's entrance into the war.[6] As World War II approached, Becker was again assailed by doubts; as before, however, he yielded to the prevailing views of his countrymen.[7]

In the Fascist countries, all scholars did not automatically come to the defense of the government. In Germany, Hitler did not win the support of Friedrich Meinecke;[8] and in Italy, Mussolini did not win the approval of Benedetto Croce.[9] To Croce, Italian fascism was a "sport" of the political process and must perish. One of the most heroic of the German historians whose liberalism ran afoul of Nazism was Veit Valentin, professor-archivist, who was deprived of his position because of his views and was, from 1933 until his death, an exile in the free atmosphere of England and the United States.[10]

For all their stress upon the relationship of historical study to good citizenship, historians generally have eschewed active politics.

In the case of historians in teaching positions, the terms of employment, if not their personal inclinations, often militate against political activity. But despite the objectivity cult which teaches that politics is highly subjective and that a historian cannot become a politician and remain a scholar, academic historians in the 1960's were represented both in the United States Senate and on the roster of politically appointed presidential advisers. Although two historians, one an amateur, the other a professional, became presidents of the United States, the first, Theodore Roosevelt, had not achieved a reputation as a scholar, and the second, Woodrow Wilson, had previously abandoned historianship for university administration, which in turn was followed by the New Jersey governorship.

One of the boldest suggestions ever made by a responsible non-academic historian that the American Historical Association itself should assume an active role in politics, was that by Charles Francis Adams (1835–1915) in his presidential address before the Association in December, 1901. Entitled, "An Undeveloped Function," the address surveyed national political campaigns from 1856 forward and concluded that most of these had been badly handled. Since historians were not only Democrats and Republicans but also scholars accustomed to the weighing and assessing of evidence, Adams recommended that a special meeting of the Association be held in July of every presidential-election year and that the issues of the campaign be discussed at this meeting. Such a meeting would serve to get the real issues of the campaign before the people, something which he thought politicians often failed to do, and would also provide an example of how these issues could be debated by sensible men. The net result, Adams thought, would be an improvement of the American political process.[11]

The notion that a knowledge of history is necessary or is at least conducive to good citizenship, has long been held and probably is the first of the assumed values of historical study which comes to mind. The American Historical Association's "Committee of Seven" which made a report in 1898 on history in the schools, thought that one of the values of history was promotion of "good and useful citizenship" and, further, that history pupils should understand that "society is in movement . . . and that in the process of change virtue must be militant if it is to be triumphant." [12] A dozen years later, the Association's Committee of Five" reported in a similar vein. History should give pupils "an appreciation of the present and a sense of social life and social responsibility. . . ."[13] And a highly respected guide-book for studying American history proclaimed historical study to be "the best training for administrative duties, for citizenship, for public life, and especially for the discussion of any question which needs a knowledge of the past for its settlement." [14]

And yet the idea that historical study has a necessary relationship to good citizenship has been challenged at a high professional level. Professor Rolla M. Tryon, who, after taking a doctorate in history, gave his chief attention to the teaching aspects of the subject, has stated flatly that "No one . . . has ever been able to prove by means of objective data that history has any value in the education of youth." Tryon submits that until studies have been made of attitudes by persons who have studied history as a school subject and of those who have not, claims for a good-citizenship connection for the subject cannot be established.[15]

The citizenship angle of historical study has left many a historian as skeptical as Tryon, although perhaps for a different reason. For once it is admitted that there is a positive relationship between the two, the temptation to write history so as to produce desirable citizenship effects, may be great. This could result ultimately in a "rigged" type of history produced by "do-gooders." This possibility may have been in the mind of Edward Eggleston when he wrote from Washington to Herbert B. Adams declining an invitation to speak before Adams's students at Johns Hopkins University. With the outbreak of the Spanish-American War only a few days away, Eggleston seems to have had a jaundiced view of his fellow-countrymen's citizenship. He told Adams that he would not speak on citizenship. "I dont [sic] care for historical study for the sake of American citizenship." "Living right at the door of Congress in this tiresome time," he added, "I don't seem to care for American citizenship; it is a brand that covers a discouraging lot of clap-trap" and "the study of history with reference to it has made half a nation irrational jingoes." [16]

This letter has a double interest: it provides insight into Eggleston's thinking about history and citizenship, and it also could have been a thrust at Adams himself as one of the "irrational jingoes." For on February 18, 1898, in his Phi Beta Kappa address at the College of William and Mary, Adams had raised the question whether the *Maine* disaster in Havana Harbor was "an accident" or a "foul deed." While he conceded that "we know not yet," he nevertheless referred to the tragedy as "this monstrous wrong, this terrible calamity in a friendly foreign port. . . ." Further, in language which would have done credit to such tub-thumpers as Theodore Roosevelt and Albert Jeremiah Beveridge, Adams said that "America is not untried in war," and asserted that "We have twice conquered England, now the greatest empire the world has seen." [17] This last observation was not owing to any current difficulties with England but was made to remind listeners of America's martial prowess.

But without reference to the Spanish-American War, it was in the late nineteenth century that the social sciences are said to have had their "Heroic Age." It was then that economists, such as Richard T. Ely and John R. Commons; sociologists, such as Lester F. Ward, and E. A. Ross; and historians, such as Herbert B. Adams, Frederick J. Turner, and Andrew D. White, all could agree that their disciplines had a social usefulness.[18] And early in the next century James Harvey Robinson was to proclaim a "new history" which would avail itself of the findings of anthropology, economics, psychology, and sociology to help men meet their "daily needs." [19]

THE HISTORIAN AND MORAL RESPONSIBILITY

There has been wide agreement among historians that their professional duties do not include the pointing of morals or the formulation of value judgments. Yet, for all their claims to objectivity, historians do make value judgments and do take moral positions. That these practices are indulged in is almost as widely recognized as the abstract principle that they are no part of historianship. Often the value judgment is made by indirection—through the use of "loaded" words and phrases, through subtle omissions, and through a between-the-lines approach; and it is conceivable that in some instances the writer is hardly aware that he has departed from the path of impartial scholarship.

The whole trouble regarding value judgments began, so critics of historianship aver, with the view that the historian cannot be as other men, but must be objective: he must discover facts and arrange them in intelligible order and then let them speak for themselves. The idea that historians should avoid making moral judg-

ments is deplored by many scholars. Thus, Sir Isaiah Berlin, professor of social and political theory at Oxford, while agreeing that
it is all right up to a point for the historian to be a detective rather
than a judge, observes that this kind of objectivity leaves the reader,
"who has none of the professional responsibilities of the expert,"
to "form what moral conclusions he likes." Objectivity in history,
says Sir Isaiah, must not be assumed "literally," because "it depends
upon a false analogy with some among the more exact of the natural
sciences." That is, since history is not a science in the sense that
chemistry is, historians are not precluded by the nature of their
subject from expressing opinions.[20]

If it is true, as Miss C. V. Wedgwood says it is, that the historian at some point becomes "aware of the desire to say that such
a thing was good or bad, such an action right or wrong," and that
the historian, possessed of beliefs and opinions as a result of his
past, cannot avoid making value judgments,[21] it is indeed a proper
question whether it would not be better to make these judgments
openly rather than by indirection. For after all, the form in which
a moral judgment is expressed is itself a moral judgment and one
unlikely to escape the intelligent reader's notice. The fullness and
universality of history make it an especially tempting source in
which to seek "lessons" and "truths." New York University philosophy professor Marie Collins Swabey, assuming that history is not
a science, suggests "that history proves that anything can be proved
by history. . . ." This is owing to the fact that "the record of the
world's events is essentially constructed by human minds and as
such shares the conflicting variety of perspectives that gave them
birth." [22] And it is for this reason that the historian, not wishing
to shirk an assumed moral responsibility, may ultimately find himself in a situation far worse than if he had remained content to be
a mere discoverer of evidence. For as Professor Swabey says, the
historical record bears the imprint of human minds that have been
formed and influenced by a variety of factors.

Granted that there is a place for the moralist in our society, the
question at issue is whether the historian should cast himself in
this role. Herbert Butterfield, differing sharply from Lord Acton
in the matter, is dubious of the historian as moralist; better assem-
ble the materials of history, he thinks, and let God be the judge
of men and events.[23] Once the historian becomes a moralist, he
may find himself pulled this way and that by parties seeking his

support, and end by using his craft to help defeat causes which should have his assistance, and vice versa. Alfred North Whitehead has testified that "in human society the champions of morality are on the whole the fierce opponents of new ideals." [24] And John Dewey has noted that "our moral beliefs are a product of the social environment," and that "in a static order, efforts at change," such as "votes for women" and "abolishing war" are said to be " 'unnatural.' " [25]

Although from the foregoing it might seem that moralizing might well be left to clergymen and philosophers, there is a persistent idea that history contains moral lessons and that it is the duty of the historian to disclose them. François P. G. Guizot said that "history is a great school of truth, reason, and virtue." [26] And English bishop and constitutional historian William Stubbs was of the opinion that "the study of modern history is, next to theology itself, and only next in so far as theology rests on a divine revelation, the most thoroughly religious training that the mind can conceive." [27]

Despite numerous disclaimers, there is implicit in much that historians have said and written the view that history has moral connotations and that historians therefore have moral responsibilities different from those of other persons. This idea is inferred, for instance, by assertions that history should promote good citizenship. The latter view was espoused by the American Historical Association's "Committee of Seven" who wished youth to gain an appreciation for social change and to see "that in the processes of change *virtue must be militant* if it is to be triumphant." [28]

Of the six "laws of history" which University of Pennsylvania Professor Edward P. Cheyney announced in 1923, one was a law of moral progress.[29] Long before Cheyney spoke, however, English historian James A. Froude had said: "One lesson, and only one, history may be said to repeat with distinctness: that the world is built somehow on moral foundations; that, in the long run, it is well with the good; in the long run, it is ill with the wicked. But this is no science; it is no more than the old doctrine taught long years ago by the Hebrew prophets." [30] Differing from Cheyney, and possibly from Froude, Cambridge University historian John B. Bury expressed the opinion that evolution does not necessarily mean a movement of society toward "a desirable goal," and that the belief in the idea of progress, moral or otherwise, like belief in

Providence and immortality, is something which cannot be proved and is, therefore, "an act of faith." [31]

If it be granted that there are moral values in history, a question arises whether these are fixed or changeable. Lord Acton believed they were fixed,[32] but, as we have seen, American historian Henry Charles Lea believed that concepts of morality are relative to the particular times, peoples, and countries being considered. To him, "the temporary and variable character of morals" rather than "a universal and inflexible standard" was the true principle for the historian.[33] Philosopher John Dewey was of a similar opinion. Michael Oakeshott, professor of political science in the London School of Economics, would have the historian eschew moral judgments entirely and value the past as he finds it for its own sake.[34]

This view of history has been sharply and elaborately challenged by Arnold J. Toynbee, research professor of international history in the University of London, and author of the celebrated work, *A Study of History*. Indeed, in our own day, no prominent historian has been more given to pronouncing moral judgments than he, and in some quarters these judgments have earned for Toynbee a reputation as an extremist. Thus, while he denounces in strongest terms the Nazi extermination of some 6,000,000 Jews, Toynbee equates this crime with the cruel treatment of some 750,000 Arabs by the new State of Israel, whose citizens he accuses of adopting the Nazi philosophy of a *Herrenvolk*. And, as something of a shocker, Toynbee expresses the opinion that, on Judgment Day, the greatest Nazi sin will not be adjudged to have been the destruction of millions of Jews, but an indirect result of this crime—the creation of the State of Israel.[35]

As already suggested, once the historian turns moralist, he encounters difficulties which may lead him into inconsistencies and the espousal of causes which he cannot have thoroughly appraised. Moreover, as in Toynbee's case, he may so play the part of moralist and prophet that, despite an erudition so formidable as to constitute one of the intellectual marvels of our times, his historianship may be compromised and may even be denied by critics.[36] To the question, Should not historians, like other decent citizens, be against sin and immorality? the answer can only be in the affirmative. But this does not solve the problem. The difficulty is that the words sin and immorality have no universally accepted meanings, and however righteous and moral a man may think himself to be, he may be regarded by his neighbor as both sinful and immoral. For example, prohibition and other phases of the temperance question are regarded by many persons as questions of sin and immorality; and only a short time ago, such questions as woman suffrage and the eight-hour day had for many persons a similar connotation.

The role of moralist is much more likely to be assumed by the historian when some great crisis confronts society than when the social flow is relatively quiet. War, as already suggested, always evokes much moralizing; for nations at war try to rationalize their actions in terms of righteousness and evil, morality and immorality, and, perhaps, religion and irreligion. At such a time, only "conscientious objectors" are likely to be allowed the intellectual luxury of denouncing war itself as the great evil, the great wrong, the all-encompassing immorality.

A HISTORIAN'S HISTORIAN: J. FRANKLIN JAMESON

In our consideration of historianship in its various aspects, it seems desirable at this point to particularize to a greater extent than we have been able to do heretofore and to sketch briefly the career of an American historian who may be said to have represented the best personal and professional qualities of our craft. It is believed that by well-nigh universal consent no one more worthy of this notice could have been chosen than the subject of the discussion which follows.

Historianship in America has been advanced not only by authors of authoritative monographic and other works on history, but also by scholars whose chief concern has been to effect conditions conducive to historical scholarship of the highest order. In this latter group of scholars, Dr. John Franklin Jameson (1859–1937) was preeminent.[37] Founder of no school of history, and author of only a modest amount of historical writing, Jameson was nevertheless the "historian's historian" to a unique degree in the annals of American historiography.

A New Englander who had taken his doctorate under Herbert Baxter Adams at Johns Hopkins University and who had taught at Brown University and at the University of Chicago, Jameson turned from teaching to what was for him the more congenial and spiritually rewarding work of editor and of administrator of significant historical enterprises. As long-time editor of the *American Historical Review,* as director of the Department of Historical Research of the Carnegie Institution of Washington, and as director of the Manuscript Division of the Library of Congress, Jameson made his influence felt in many ways upon the cause of historical scholarship. In addition to stimulating the calendaring of American historical materials in foreign archives, serving as supervising editor of materials on early American history, assembling a staff to edit collections of documents on various significant phases of American history, and maintaining the highest standards for the *Review,* Dr. Jameson, through correspondence and other contacts, encouraged such large enterprises as the editing of Washington's writings, the production of the *Dictionary of American Biography,* and the establishment of the National Archives. The latter was an undertaking of the highest priority with him and was urged upon Presidents Taft and Wilson and later statesmen.[38]

Dr. Jameson's correspondence embraced the names of a wide sample of leading historians of his time and of many men in public life so situated as to be able to assist historical scholarship. A selection of his correspondence includes letters to Henry Adams, Charles M. Andrews, Charles A. Beard, Carl Becker, James Bryce, William E. Dodd, Max Farrand, Albert Bushnell Hart, Charles H. Haskins, Andrew C. McLaughlin, Dana C. Munro, H. Morse Stephens, George M. Trevelyan, Frederick J. Turner, Woodrow Wilson, and many others. His letters to Wilson began when the two men were colleagues in the historical profession and mutually concerned with such matters as textbooks and professional meetings, and bore the salutation, "My dear Wilson." The correspondence was continued on a more formal basis during Wilson's Presidency of the United States.

A gentleman of the old school, handsomely bearded and of impressive appearance, Dr. Jameson possessed warm personal qualities and a sense of humor that belied an austere exterior. A young researcher in manuscripts in the Carnegie Institution of Washington during a Christmas holiday season, after calling out a "Merry Christmas" to Dr. Jameson, was surprised when, instead of giving a conventional response, the distinguished scholar rose from his desk, walked across the room, and grasped the young man by the hand to say "Thank you." Yet this courtly gentleman enjoyed writing light verse that sparkled with fun. And although he described himself as "an old Federalist . . . of the Adams-Bayard-Marshall variety," [39] Jameson was not reactionary. Doubting Woodrow Wilson's judgment in handling senatorial opposition to the Treaty of Versailles,[40] Jameson at the same time was in sympathy with the President's major objectives. At a later date, like many citizens of both parties, he was disturbed at Franklin Roosevelt's court-packing plan and took a skeptical view of congressional and popular judgment on matters of constitutionality.[41] Moreover, Dr. Jameson had no tolerance for persons who wished school histories to omit important facts which certain citizens might dislike—such facts, for example, as those about the Russian Revolution—and he strongly defended Carl Becker's high-school history of modern Europe on this score.[42] Much earlier still, he had become a champion of academic freedom by heading a faculty protest at Brown University against the resignation of President E. Benjamin Andrews, caused by differences between the economic views of Andrews and the governing board. Nor did Jameson allow his "old Federalist" bias to becloud his judgment of American political history. Well before the turn of the century, he stated his belief that the American people, by virtue of their background, were predominantly democratic and that in elections they veered from the Democratic political path and formed opposing parties for temporary corrective purposes only.[43]

Despite a New England background, Dr. Jameson had early aspired to write a history of the South as a major work; this he never did, although his editing of Calhoun correspondence, and his part in having published such works as the records of the Virginia Company, and judicial cases concerning American Negro slavery, testified to his continuing interest in the section. Author of learned introductions, prefaces, and articles, Jameson's best-known book was *The American Revolution Considered as a Social Movement*. But abandoning teaching in mid-career and not having time for prolific writings, Jameson, as noted, founded no school of history; instead, he labored mightily and successfully to facilitate the work of the entire historical fraternity. Early in his professional career he became convinced that American historiography was not to be advanced entirely by brilliant writers such as Henry Adams and Francis Parkman, and felt that an era of spadework by historical specialists would have a wholesome effect upon American historiography.[44] No coddler of the mediocre, Jameson nevertheless saw that the brilliant synthesizers and interpreters could do their work only after a vast amount of research and monographic writing had been done by others, many of them of average talents. Without this basic research, American historiography, what with the rapidly growing volume of documentary and other materials for history, might be ever so impressive in style and yet be shallow in quality. It was thus as a catalytic agent in bringing historians of varied qualities and interests into working relationships with historical materials that Jameson's greatest work was done. His own distinguished writing, although not formidable in volume, showed how fruitful this process could be.

V

THE GROWING COMPLEXITY
OF HISTORIANSHIP

WHEN HE IS in a lazy mood the historian cannot but look with nostalgia upon those earlier days of his craft when history was regarded as being essentially a political story, garnished with asides on constitutional, diplomatic, and military developments. Indeed, if he told well the political story alone, stark and unadorned, the historian needed have no fears for his reputation as a scholar. Not that many historians took literally the Edward A. Freeman dictum that history and past politics were one and the same thing; polite recognition of non-political phases of history was common among historians even before the turn of the century. But in the actual practice of historianship—research, writing, and teaching—political history was history. If pressed, probably most historians would have admitted that they thought social history too inconsequential and frivolous to be made a part of history courses and of written history. They might also have noted that the materials of social history are more difficult to come by than are those of political history.

HISTORY'S LOSSES TO OTHER DISCIPLINES

One of the earliest histories of the United States which showed subject-matter balance was not written by an American historian at all but by geographer-historian Hugh Murray, Fellow of the Royal Society of Edinburgh. The history was in three volumes and was published seventeen years before the outbreak of the American Civil War. The work was notable not only for its balance and restraint, even in treating so controversial a subject as the American Revolution, but also for the research upon which it was based. It was notable also for its tabular material and documentation, and for its breadth of treatment. The author observed that he used materials which had escaped certain earlier writers "and were inaccessible to the still more diligent researches of Mr. Bancroft." [1] His citations include references to travellers' accounts and to pamphlets in the British Museum and to documents published by Congress. As an example of restrained interpretation may be noted Murray's treatment of the Declaration of Independence where he anticipated Claude H. Van Tyne and Carl Becker by many years. Thus, Murray calls attention to the Declaration's imputation of guilt to the King and its omission of mention of Parliament, and notes that it ignored the real causes. He correctly pointed out that "arbitrary taxation, and the alteration of charters, occupied only a secondary place" in the document.[2]

Over a fourth of Volume II is devoted to agriculture, commerce, and other subjects apart from political-diplomatic-military history. And nearly all of Volume III is given over to manners and social life, slaves and slavery, religion, literature, emigration, and the geology, topography, botany, and zoology of the country. Altogether, of the some 1150 pages in the three volumes, about 40 percent represent social, economic, and cultural history, which is about the percentage allotted these subjects by the better present-day college textbooks on United States history.

But historians in the United States did not enlarge their vision of history until much of the neglected areas had been preempted by other disciplines. Even political history, regarded as the very backbone of history, suffered from heavy inroads made by political science. As a mounting volume of books on government—local, state, national, and international—all interlarded and buttressed with historical facts, products of political science seemed very closely akin to the work that historians were doing. As for this, it was not unusual for a given scholar to work in both fields, and the roster of these ambivalent workers contained such distinguished names as those of Woodrow Wilson, John W. Burgess, and Charles A. Beard.

In economic history, the writings of such able economists as Davis R. Dewey, Frank W. Taussig, and John R. Commons suggested that another significant segment of history was to be lost by professional historians. Economists, however, soon became so engrossed with the numerous specialties they developed that to some extent the historical phases of their subject—general economic history and the history of economic thought—were left to scholars trained primarily as historians, not as economists.

Educational history, even more than governmental and economic history, fell to non-professional historians. Education professors E. B. Cubberley and Paul Monroe gained renown after the turn of the century for their histories of American education, and, with some exceptions, professional historians have until recently seemed willing to allow educationists to dominate this field. True, professional historians often had in their general works some material on educational history; likely as not, however, this was but a rehash of standard accounts by educationists rather than a product of fresh and independent research. Even in our own day, professional historians, such as Richard Hofstadter, Frederick Rudolph, and George P. Schmidt, who turn to educational history are likely to limit their investigations to colleges and universities and thus develop a significant segment, but only a segment, of the whole story. The fact is that "education," in the sense of educationist education, has become an unpopular word among subject-matter specialists, most of whom feel that it connotes a low order of scholarship.

The field of intellectual history the historians have shared with philosophers and professors of English and American literature. Since literature comprises so much of the source material for intellectual history, it was perhaps inevitable that intellectual history should be found in large measure in works produced by members of university English staffs. Among works of this kind may be mentioned those of William P. Trent and Vernon L. Parrington. Professional historians who have contributed significantly to American intellectual history include Merle Curti, S. E. Morison, Ralph H. Gabriel, Perry Miller, Thomas J. Wertenbaker, and Henry S. Commager. Professor Harvey Wish, in a work of wider scope than those produced by the foregoing authors, has devoted much space to intellectual history, and so have Charles A. and Mary Beard in a work of wider scope still. Natural scientist and historian John William Draper likewise gave attention to intellectual history but sought his theme outside the United States.[3]

HISTORY AND THE BEHAVIORAL SCIENCES

But it is with reference to sociology and the behavioral sciences that historians face their greatest difficulties. To attempt to participate in these specialties on a research basis is, to the historian, unthinkable. Even to borrow intelligently the findings made by social scientists, however, involves problems of judgment and of some familiarity with the scope and personnel of the behavioral sciences. What, then, is the historian to do about the growing number of social science specialties that impinge on history and whose processes rely somewhat upon the findings of history? Is the result to be—as Johns Hopkins University philosopher Arthur O. Lovejoy recommended it should be—a cooperative history with numerous specialists in history, philosophy, and social sciences contributing to each segment of the story? Or is it to be, as natural scientist Alexis Carrel advised, the product of a single, widely informed mind? [5]

On the basis of present knowledge, Lovejoy's seems the more plausible of the two approaches. For Lovejoy is not recommending the kind of cooperative approach we have in the *Cambridge Modern History,* where a segment is turned over to a specialist, but rather an approach in which each segment itself would be treated cooperatively by associated scholars. Individual writers who have tried to encompass the entire field have not been very successful. Even Arnold J. Toynbee, with his brilliance and vast erudition, fell short of bringing together all that must be included in any comprehensive study of history. Toynbee recognizes clearly the problems posed for historians by the social and behavioral sciences and understands that historians can ill afford to allow these disciplines to take from history all that intelligent readers may think meaningful in it.[6] Yet social scientist Pitirim Sorokin has shown that Toynbee was insufficiently acquainted with social sciences for his great undertaking and that he expended much time and space on problems already better handled by social scientists.[7]

But, as Toynbee suggests, if historians wash their hands of the social and behavioral sciences, history may become more and more a spade-work or hod-carrying discipline serving social scientists who are unafraid to use and interpret facts turned up by historians' labors. Try as he may, however, the historian's problem in keeping abreast of what auxiliary sciences may be doing that has relevance for history is a very considerable one. Thus, a recent work surveying the status of sociology, published under the auspices of the American Sociological Society,[8] treats of such subspecialties as political sociology, the sociology of law, the sociology of education, the sociology of religion, and the sociology of art, science, and medicine. Moreover, the overall subject is concerned with urban, rural, and industrial sociology, with the sociology of race, and with occupations, demographic behavior, and social stratification. To take a practical example, if the historian seeks to know something of political sociology, he discovers immediately that he has a problem of selection among authorities. He will find several specialists in the field on the faculties of American universities, and as he looks further he will encounter names of European contributors, such as Émile Durkheim, Vilfredo Pareto, and Max Weber.[9] Much the same situation will confront him wherever he turns in the social sciences and their subspecialties, and because of the sheer bulk of the bibliography and its specialized character, he must, perforce, rely upon syntheses by the appropriate specialists. But these syntheses will not completely solve his problem, since he still must know who speaks authoritatively for the majority of scholars in any given specialty. As Clyde Kluckhohn has shown for his own field of anthropology, opinions among his colleagues vary widely on such matters as morals, values, absolutes, and universals.[10]

It is being increasingly recognized by historians that psychology has much to offer them in the area of interpretation. Social psychologists' studies of leadership, revolution, war and morale, public opinion, and psychological warfare all impinge on history.[11] The psychology of Sigmund Freud is especially important, for, according to David Riesman, "it is Freud and his followers who have had the principal impact on American social science. . . ." This has been especially true in the area of " 'culture and personality' studies" and in cultural anthropology.[12] Interpretations of such subjects as art and religion, both of which come within the historian's province, can scarcely avoid Freud.[13] Carl Gustav Jung likewise enters the world of historianship, as is evidenced by Toynbee's *A Study of History*, which was much influenced by Jung's theories.[14] Even if the historian puts to one side theories of dreams and of the psyche as espoused by Jung, the latter's study of "extroverts" and "introverts" contains suggestions for anyone trying to interpret man and his actions.[15] Goodwin Watson avers that since both the historian and the psychologist are concerned with "human behavior," the difference between them is, to some extent, the "size of the sample" studied.[16]

To take a single example of the relationship between history and psychology, there is perhaps in all American history no topic more in need of the services of psychoanalysis for its complete understanding than the public-service role of the Adams family. Brilliant, unusually upright and patriotic, and of great service to their country, the Adamses were nevertheless so self-centered and egotistical as to measure the progress or retrogression of the nation in terms of their own political fortunes. In their view, the country started on the downgrade when President John Adams, standing for re-election in 1800, was defeated by Thomas Jefferson, and its ruination was made well-nigh complete when President John Quincy Adams, standing for re-election in 1828, was defeated by Andrew Jackson.[17] Since from near 1850 forward, the Adamses, excepting Charles Francis, Sr., counted for but little in public life, it was not surprising that able historians Henry Adams and Brooks Adams should have been so pessimistic about the America of the late nineteenth and early twentieth centuries. John Adams's most recent and authoritative biographer has noted the psychoanalytical problems involved in understanding John and his wife, Abigail; and similar problems seem to be involved in understanding certain others of the family, notably John Quicy Adams and his grandson Henry Adams. In analyzing the conduct of John Adams, the biographer of the "Duke of Braintree" speaks of traits of the "Puritan" and the "hedonist," and uses such words as "paranoid," "schizophrenic," and "manic-depressive," and other terms peculiar to psychoanalysis.[18]

Upon archaeology also, the dependence of history for certain types of specialized knowledge has long been recognized. And anthropology, both physical and cultural, likewise makes a large contribution to an understanding of man and his past. Indian civilizations of North and South America, their origins and characteristics, were first systematically studied by archaeologists and anthropologists. An example of this contribution is found in the valuable research findings on man in early America by Aleš Hrdlička,[19] founder of the American Association of Physical Anthropologists.

In view of the foregoing survey, brief as it is, one can appreciate the remark of Alfred Cobban, professor of French history, University College, London, who, noting the influence of economics on history, said that "Other forms of social science will also need to be called on . . if general history is to retain significance, and if it is to continue to be a valid instrument of education, and an activity worthy of the attention of intelligent men and women." [20] The process which Cobban recommends here would involve the kind of social science synthesis that Harvard philosopher Morton White has called "cultural organicism." [21]

AMERICAN HISTORIANSHIP COMES FULL CYCLE

As all historians know, one of the easiest errors that can be made is to assume that a particular idea is "new." Relatively few ideas are really new, and some ideas now thought to be new were current in ancient times. The scientific historical method commonly regarded as being a product of modern times was practiced by Thucydides during the fifth century, B.C.; and the concept of history as an all-encompassing account of man's past—a concept now being advanced in the pages of learned historical magazines— was brilliantly advocated and followed by Ibn Khaldûn of Tunis, over five-and-a-half centuries ago. Ordericus Vitalis' twelfth-century account of England and Normandy, despite many glaring defects, had much historical merit and was rich in what is nowadays called social history.[22]

During the last quarter of the nineteenth century the general preference in the United States was for political history (the *Staatengeschichte* of Ranke). Significantly, the statement of English historian Edward A. Freeman that "History is past Politics and Politics present History" hung on the wall in the history-seminar room at Johns Hopkins. Nevertheless, there was some conception of a more comprehensive history. Herbert B. Adams, for instance, who followed but did not introduce the seminar method at Hopkins,[23] was keenly aware of history's connections with archaeology, geography, economics, statistics, and political economy. Adams said that he had never taught history according to the Freeman dictum, "but only that some history and some politics" could be explained by it. "It must be fully recognized," he said, "that history is past religion, past philosophy, past civilization, past sociology, and includes all man's recorded action and experience in organized society. . . ." [24]

Moreover, Professor Ephraim Emerton of Harvard, in discussing desirable requirements for the doctorate in American universities, recommended in 1893 that the student have undergraduate training in philosophy, economics, and the fine arts, and in several languages. "Taking the languages in order of importance," said Emerton, the prospective graduate student of history "ought to make himself able to read easily Latin, German, and French, and should have some knowledge of Greek." Upon completion of college, he should be able to "handle without great difficulty materials, original and second hand, in a half-dozen languages." Since Emerton did not regard "the science of historical evidence" as "an exact science," and he felt the element of probability in history was large, he believed that judgment must necessarily be an important quality of the historian. Presumably, he thought the training he recommended would help supply this need.[25]

But despite pioneering efforts to give history a wider context, the first significant movement in the United States to remove the subject from its political-history mold was not made until the early part of the twentieth century when James Harvey Robinson launched his conception of a "new history." Through his teaching at Barnard and Columbia, through his textbooks, and especially through his book, *The New History,* published in 1912, Robinson advanced his view that history's primary obligation was to the present and urged that history avail itself of findings in its auxiliary subjects—economics and the behavioral sciences. The progress made in American social history during the past half-century has, to a large extent, been directly influenced by Robinson's writings, and it has been indirectly influenced by him through such students of his as Arthur M. Schlesinger and Dixon Ryan Fox and their doctoral candidates in history.[26]

During the 1920's, the large role that Robinson had envisaged for historians received new emphasis when the Social Science Research Council was organized and historians were brought into close cooperation with specialists in disciplines having relevance for history. Professor Roy F. Nichols has shown that this new development caused some historians to wonder just what their identity was: Were they humanists or social scientists, or something in between? [27]

The concepts of Adams, Emerton, and Robinson, especially of the first two, did not go as far as the recommendations of certain historians of the present day. There is now increasing insistence that historians should know more than they do about anthropology, psychology, sociology, and economics, and further, that they should give more attention to the history of education. Intellectual and literary history also make their claims.[28] If man is the proper subject of history, and if, as Boyd C. Shafer has said, the likenesses of men need to be given greater attention than their differences, then the behavioral sciences and other studies that help explain man's nature cannot be neglected by historians. But historians cannot so extend their interests without creating problems for themselves. Professor Leonard Krieger has pointed out that if the historian enters new fields, he becomes "a hyphenated historian," that is, "a philosopher-historian" or "a sociologist-historian" or some other academic compound, whereas if he adheres to the time-and-change functions of historianship, he remains an "autonomous historian." Krieger notes that the historian is "inevitably" of both types.[30] Within the behavioral sciences themselves, similar problems have arisen. Columbia University anthropologist Ralph Linton (1893–1953) observed that researches of anthropologists, psychologists, and sociologists were so closely related that they could no longer stand completely alone, each discipline to itself. Yet the necessary collaboration was limited by specialization and subject-matter semantics.[31]

So far as this writer is aware, the boldest proposal ever advanced by a prominent historian for a close affiliation of historianship with other specialties was made by Professor William L. Langer in his presidential address before the American Historical Association in December, 1957. Apparently impressed by the uses made of Freudian psychology by other subject-matter specialists, Langer appealed to historians to substitute for their own apathetic or hostile attitudes toward the subject, and for their amateur excursions into the field, a more serious study of psychoanalysis and "depth psychology," as a means of reaching a better understanding of man, individually and collectively. Langer noted that anthropologists, sociologists, and certain other specialists in the social sciences and humanities had attended psychoanalytic institutes for training, and he suggested "that some of our own younger men might seek the same equipment." [32]

Whether the coming generation of historians become "new" historians and secure training in psychoanalytic institutes or not, it seems clear, both from the recommendations of eminent historians and from the broader approach to history evidenced in many current histories, that the task of historianship has grown in complexity many fold since the days when political history was dominant. These developments indicate that American historianship is about to complete full cycle—that it is about to return to the ideals of certain historians at the close of the nineteenth century, who saw, for all the talk of Rankean *Staatengeschichte,* that history could not be dissociated from its allied subjects. The most authentic precursors of the new historiography, however, were not historians at all, but sociologists and economists, notably Lester F. Ward and Thorstein Veblen, both of whom were unusual for their wide grasp of subjects, scientific and non-scientific, that had significant relevance for their own studies.[33] More recently, sociologist Karl Mannheim has attempted an integration of the social sciences.[34]

If the new historiography is to be taken seriously, a practical question in education inevitably arises: Where are the men and women to be found who can gain sufficient mastery of history's allies to be useful, and at the same time acquire the necessary mastery of one or more fields of history? At a time when there is considerable feeling that the time requirements for the doctorate must be strictly limited, when there is even debate whether a reading knowledge of both French and German should be required for the doctorate, and when it is being said that history doctoral candidates must be given some preparation for teaching,[35] implications of the new historiography for graduate departments of history are staggering. The tasks suggested for aspiring historians by Ephraim Emerton, including acquisition of a working knowledge of a half-dozen foreign languages, may seem simple compared with the problem of acquiring a working competence in Freudian psychology and in several additional fields of the social sciences and the humanities —all of which would, of course, have to be added to a graduate program in history proper. May it not be that the impossible is being proposed, and that the most that can be hoped for is intelligent cooperation between historians and specialists in the humanities and behavioral sciences, including thoughtful borrowings, the one from the others. As James Schouler had the wit to see long ago— if we may repeat his statement at the conclusion of our Chapter Two—"In the present age one must be ignorant of much if he would be proficient in something." [36]

VI

THE PREPARATION AND PRACTICE
OF THE HISTORIAN

THE ORTHODOX PATH leading to historianship begins with an undergraduate major in history and continues through a graduate department of history. There the student is taught certain methods of research and writing and he studies several fields of history, one or two of them in some depth. The prospective historian secures the preliminary accolade of historianship when, upon completion of an approved course of study, the presentation of an acceptable dissertation, and the passing of a searching examination, he is awarded the degree of doctor of philosophy.

LAUNCHING A HISTORICAL CAREER

With his doctoral diploma as certification of his basic competence as a student of history, and with the backing of his graduate department, our new historian probably will secure a position as a teacher in a college or university. If he does not enter teaching, he may secure an archival, editorial, administrative, or other position in which he can use his training in historianship to good advantage. If he enters teaching he is likely to begin as an instructor, and either in the institution of his initial appointment or in institutions to which he subsequently moves, he will normally make his way upward through the ranks of assistant professor and associate professor, and finally become a professor of full rank. He may begin his teaching career at a rank above that of instructor, depending upon the employing institution. As a teacher, the historian will offer instruction in a fixed schedule of courses, including, he hopes, at least one closely related to his specialty. And from time to time he is likely to write articles and books treating critically some phase of history and also to prepare for learned journals reviews of books written by fellow historians.

But the foregoing procedures are only the conventional way to historianship. It was a way largely unknown in the United States before the last quarter of the nineteenth century. It was not the route followed by Motley, Parkman, and Prescott, except in scholarly productivity, for during their youth there were no graduate departments of history. Nor was it the way of some later historical writers who attained prominence. Henry Charles Lea and James Ford Rhodes turned to history after first successfully pursuing business careers. Albert J. Beveridge, lawyer and United States Senator, won renown in American history and biography, especially for his *Life of John Marshall*. Several journalistic writers have likewise achieved success as historians and biographers.

Granted that they have aptitude for getting at important facts and weighing evidence, the clue to the success of historical writers who have not undergone the rigorous discipline of graduate historical instruction may lie in their ability to write unusually well. This is a quality which graduate instruction rarely imparts, and it is a quality whose lack has done much to confine academic historianship to academic circles and cause it to be ignored by a large and intelligent reading public. It even has been charged that some graduate departments, instead of improving students' writing style, actually impair it. This impairment results, it is said, from graduate schools' heavy emphasis upon scientific method and objectivity, which discourages any native flair for vivid expression students may have. The non-academic historian, runs the theory, unencumbered by graduate school taboos, writes in whatever manner his judgment directs and without inhibiting his style by a cult of objectivity. In some instances, to borrow a phrase from Carl Becker, he may "write without fear and without research." [1] Nevertheless, because of heavy borrowings from academic historians, he may state most of his facts accurately. These he probably will interpret subjectively. The relatively enthusiastic way in which writings of this kind are received by the public, and by a considerable percentage of academic historians as well, evinces a widespread desire of readers to have not only facts but also the writer's opinion of them.

Academic historians are not of one mind as to the need for special methodology courses in the preparation of prospective historians, and this disagreement may encourage the belief that historianship is something that any person of common sense can master. In his presidential address before the American Historical Association in 1950, Samuel Eliot Morison spoke scathingly of historical methodology courses and of historians who offer them. "Historical methodology, as I see it," said he, "is a product of common sense applied to circumstances." [2] Even in 1926 Allen Johnson must have had the prevalence of some such view in mind when he wrote in the Preface of his *The Historian and Historical Evidence:* "To those who believe that literary cleverness and common sense are the only needful equipment for a historian, this book will seem a work of supererogation." [3] But that present-day historical methodology courses enjoy better standing than Professor Morison's remarks might seem to indicate, was shown by Louis R. Gottschalk in his presidential address before the Association in 1953.[4]

HISTORY AS A "PROFESSION"

The fact that journalists, businessmen, lawyers, and statesmen are able to enter the field of historical writing and earn substantial reputations as historians may suggest strongly that historianship is not a "profession" in the usual sense of the term. For after all, members of the foregoing groups cannot, without undergoing specialized preparation, enter the profession of medicine, or engineering, or law, or even of public school teaching. In the main, a profession is characterized by protective bastions, legal and extra-legal, to prevent its practice by persons of inadequate preparation. The practice of medicine, for example, is controlled by state regulatory authority, and preparation for it is tightly supervised by the accrediting branch of the American Medical Association. Similar safeguards are found in law and engineering and in numerous other professions.

Although Philip Guedalla insisted that a "professional" historian is one who makes his living by writing history, most historians probably will agree with Richard Pares that the real professional is one who makes his living as a professor of the subject.[5] For, as we are trying to show in this chapter, the practice of historianship includes much more than the writing of history, important as that activity is.

As a distinct branch of the college curriculum, history amounted to but little before the year 1875, and it came into its own only after about 1900. As late as 1880, "There were only eleven professors of history in the United States";[6] and at the University of Nebraska, "when a Chair of History was established . . . grave professors, educated under the old order of things, regarded it as an unwarranted expenditure of time and money. History should, they thought, be made auxiliary to some other department." [7] At that time the view was common that history should be taught in connection with philosophy or be included in political economy or some other composite course.

The tardiness with which history arrived as an independent discipline is indicated by the fact that the American Historical Association was not organized until 1884 and the *American Historical Review* was not launched until 1895. Even recently, John H. Randall, Jr. has suggested that if academic teaching were rationally organized, there would be no need for departments of history as such, since the subject-matter of every college department has a history and therefore each department should have a historian as well as a philosopher.[8]

At the college level, "professional" standards in history are maintained informally and voluntarily. In effect, this means that history departmental heads who, with occasional exceptions, have been prepared as historians in graduate schools, make appointments to their staffs from men and women similarly prepared. This guarantees that historians on college and university faculties will have much in common—not so much in subject-matter, for this will vary with specialization—but in their outlook on their calling, its methods, standards, and responsibilities. For all practical purposes, then, as Pares has said, when we speak of the "history profession," we have reference to the men and women who teach history in colleges and universities. It may seem ironical that this should be so, for the pedagogical side of historianship is perhaps its least appealing feature to a large segment of its present and prospective practitioners.

The rise of history to an established position in the curriculum of higher education has been a matter of the greatest importance to the cause of historical research and writing. For without this assured curricular position, most of the history being written today probably would be either by persons who had gained a competence in some other calling and then turned to history, or by persons who could afford time from their regular work to indulge an interest in it. It has been fortunate for American historiography that so many of the persons thus intellectually motivated and economically situated should also have been of high quality as historians and men. Both Parkman and Prescott, for example, worked under enormous physical handicaps; yet Parkman wrote that "if by God's mercy, a single finger is unloosed, its feeble strength will not lie idle." [9]

Henry Adams believed that historical writing in America would have to be done by men who, like himself, were economically independent. His view was not without plausibility, for Adams estimated that his own celebrated *History,* which after ten years had returned royalties of only $5,000, cost him, in time and cash outlays, $80,000.[10] Bancroft and Prescott also invested formidable sums in their histories. Fortunately for them, however, sales of their books were large and the financial returns impressive.[11] Bancroft, whose circumstances in early life were somewhat straitened, was able in his old age to engage in substantial philanthropies.[12]

With reference to finances of some early historians, it may be noted that the mailing address of John L. Motley when he was researching abroad on his Dutch history was "Baring Brothers and Co., London," [13] and that James Ford Rhodes had an address "In care of the Second National Bank, Boston." [14] Moreover, returning to the melancholy Adams, it is significant that, in a day when the dollar was worth several times what it is now and there was no income tax, except the 3-10 percent levy for the period 1861–1872, Adams had an income that may have reached $50,000 a year. With such resources he was able to have most of his *History* privately printed in an edition of six copies for reading and criticism by friends before he had it published.[15]

But the academicization of history altered the economic and social conditions of historical writing. For once history became a required school subject, teachers of school history had to be prepared by the colleges and college teachers in turn had to be prepared by graduate schools. This meant that a person wishing to write history had no longer to be economically independent. A college teaching position would supply funds for a livelihood, and research and writing could now be carried on by the teacher as an adjunct or even as an integral part of his duties to the college. Further, with the proliferation of foundations having much money to award as grants, prizes, or fellowships a sizable addition was made to the potential financial resources of college history professors who wished to write history. In a word, college payrolls and foundation largess did much to fill the historical scholarship void which Henry Adams thought could be filled only by the dividends, interest, and rents, of independently wealthy men.

Whether historianship should become a full-fledged profession is a question which cannot be considered lightly. For once a calling becomes a profession it must assume burdens and responsibilities not previously borne by it. Among these are the accrediting of institutions preparing practitioners and setting up of administrative machinery to handle accrediting operations. At present there is no effective or thoroughgoing accreditation of graduate schools.[16] Requirements for membership in associations or groupings to which graduate schools or their officials may now belong are at best of so general a character as to be meaningless respecting departments.

One may ask, Does it really matter whether a learned calling goes into accrediting operations or not? As to this, much depends upon what the calling wishes to accomplish. Some scholars may doubt that any learned calling can afford to be indifferent toward having its highest academic degree conferred by graduate schools that may lack library and personnel resources for such advanced work. This would be especially true of any ill-equipped institutions showing no promise of substantial improvement within the near future.

To say that the problem will correct itself—that is, if a department's resources are inadequate for doctoral-level work, its doctoral graduates will be unable to secure satisfactory employment and the department will consequently drop its Ph.D. program—is not very realistic. Many employers of Ph.D.'s, including the Federal Government, make little or no distinction between graduate schools. In numerous employment situations a doctorate from any one of a number of graduate schools, varying widely in quality, will meet requirements. For this reason, it is conceivable that the American

Historical Association eventually may feel obliged to reduce to accrediting standards the informal recommendations which have already been made by a study conducted under its auspices[17] and to take whatever steps may be necessary to administer the program.

Insofar as purely academic and pedagogical matters are concerned, there always has been a sharp distinction between self-taught historians and those prepared by graduate schools. The self-taught are unlikely to break into the ranks of "professorial historians." Impressive as may be their research productivity in a given area of history, self-taught historians usually lack the broad grounding in history that successful college history teaching requires. Therefore, should professorial historians resort to accrediting practices, this would be done, presumably, not because of any threat to academic historianship by self-taught historians, but for the purpose of tightening standards within the ranks of academic historians themselves and assuring a higher degree of uniformity than now exists in preparation of candidates for graduate degrees in history.

If these procedures further sharpened the distinction between academic and non-academic historians, the distinction would not be invidious. For in the past, as already noted, non-academic historians have contributed importantly to historical research literature, and it may be hoped that their research interests will be continued. It has been wholesome for academic historians to see what can be accomplished in the field of history by men and women who have not had the advantage of graduate-school training in the subject. Their work may indicate areas in current graduate-school programs that could be dispensed with or modified. If their writings suggest that certain techniques in research and writing can be mastered without benefit of expensive and time-consuming seminars, perhaps the latter could be dropped and the time thereby saved devoted to more fruitful historical study.

THE HISTORIAN AS A TEACHER

The calling of the historian is an exalted one. When he was a professor of history at Trinity College, North Carolina, John Spencer Bassett wrote that, as a historian, he was trying to do God's work.[18] The responsibility of the historian is especially heavy in the matter of teaching, for through this medium he has his best opportunity to influence the thinking of youth. As countless students have testified, this influence has often been real and enduring. Thus, a Barnard College alumna said of the teaching of James Harvey Robinson: "His last advice to us was to look at things with an open mind —not to accept blindly the godly and respectable—to be honest and just. As a result of his teachings, I have been free and uneasy all my life." [19] And Carl Becker left us a most delightful description of his student reactions to the lectures of Frederick J. Turner, his hero among historians. Wrote Becker: "I didn't care *what* he offered. For him I would even study history." [20]

As we have seen, it was an improved place for history in the college curriculum and resulting salary-based teaching positions which made it possible for history professors to pursue specialized research and writing interests. It might almost be said that it was this arrangement which enabled poor men to become historians and kept history from being merely a rich man's hobby. Although nearly everywhere the teacher-historian was expected to teach a specified number of hours per week, there was likely to be an informal agreement that he would also do research and write articles and books, preferably books. An average college might make but little of this latter commitment, whereas one of the highest standing might place great emphasis upon it. An institution engaged in graduate work, especially if it conferred the doctorate, might make research and writing a formal part of the historian's duties.

It has long been said that in some universities where many graduate degrees are conferred, "good teaching" may count for but little in winning promotions, whereas research and writing may count for nearly everything. The professor who is a productive scholar but who cannot or will not teach well may be promoted to a choice professorship and secure from his university and from foundations whatever he wants to facilitate his research. Such a professor is an object lesson to graduate students and junior faculty members alike. And another faculty member, regarded as one of the university's finest teachers but receiving only nominal salary increases or none at all, is likewise an object lesson.

More specifically, assuming that his poor performance is not owing to lack of aptitude for communication, several factors may account for a teacher's unsatisfactory instructional record. It may be that he deliberately chooses not to be a good teacher because he is unwilling to pay the price that such teaching exacts. As every professor knows, good teaching is some of the hardest work a mortal can perform. Ideas do not organize themselves automatically; factual relationships do not emerge without assistance; meaningful interpretations do not leap from the printed page; and published findings of other scholars do not reach the teacher through his mere wishing. After the necessary grubbing has been done for twelve or fifteen classroom sessions a week, perhaps representing two to four separate courses, the instructor can have but little time or energy left for work on a learned book or article. It is at this point that the object lesson of the poor teacher who is a highly rewarded, productive scholar strikes home. And so our young assistant professor, six years out of graduate school and with a wife and two children to support, concludes that good teaching simply is not worthwhile.

If he has not eschewed good teaching for the foregoing reasons, there is another circumstance which may turn a potentially fine teacher into a poor one and at the same time help ease his conscience for his choice. This circumstance partakes of the subtle and the insidious and has in it overtones of semantic difficulties and interdisciplinary prejudices. It may be analyzed somewhat as follows: "Good teaching" smacks of secondary schools and of the jargon of teachers' colleges and colleges of education; educationists, some of whom have not been renowned teachers, have been critical of teaching in liberal arts colleges; and finally, education in the sense of educationist-education is superficial and frivolous, and subject-matter specialists should avoid becoming contaminated by it in any way.

This feud between academic specialists and educationists is a striking fact when it is remembered that two former United States Commissioners of Education were among the founders of the American Historical Association, and that at the turn of the century, schoolmen and historians were able to join hands in the common undertaking of educating youth. Beginning with its celebrated Committee of Seven in the 1890's and its Committee of Five a dozen years later, both dealing with history in secondary schools, and its Committee of Eight concerned with the subject in elementary schools, the American Historical Association early showed a keen interest in subcollegiate education. And the Association has long had a Committee on Teaching. Nevertheless, the professionalization of education and the specialization of historians have largely driven the two groups apart.

THE HISTORIAN AS A PRODUCTIVE WRITER

Charles Evans Hughes said that "the Constitution is what the judges say it is," and Felix Frankfurter is reported to have said that the Supreme Court is the Constitution.[21] Substituting the words history and historians for Constitution and Supreme Court, it probably could be said with equal truth that history is whatever the historians say it is. That is, for all practical purposes, history is written history rather than the sum total of all past human acts and thoughts. As R. F. Arragon has said, "History is not what happened but an interpretation of what happened. . . ."[22] And fortunately there is not in history, as there is in law, a doctrine of *stare decisis* which makes an interpretation, once announced, semisacred. For this reason, most "definitive" works of history have to be supplanted or drastically revised within a generation.

It is a source of regret among academic historians that laymen seem so indiscriminate in their choice of historical reading material. Many books bearing the word "history" in their titles may have been written by news reporters, world travellers, philosophers, politicians, or specialists in behavioral science. The average reader is no respecter of specialties and subspecialties, however, and is likely to make his own evaluation of a work said to be history. If he finds the book well written and informative he may give it a higher rating than a dull book on the same subject by an academic historian of impeccable scholarship.

This kind of situation is distressing for two reasons: first, the non-academic work to which the reader gives his favor may be bad history—a work abounding in false analogies, oversimplifications, and conclusions unwarranted by any evidence adduced; second, the academic historian loses the contest, not because his book is bad history, but only because it is so lacking in interpretation and is so written as to cause the reader to nod after only a few pages. A dull style is a defect so serious that no amount of learned documentation sown between chapters, and no amount of publicity given the author's competence and the honors bestowed upon him by institutions and foundations (which may have financed the project) will induce Mr. Average Reader to plough through a boring book.

But one must not be unmindful of the sage opinion of the late Richard Pares that it is not so much the historian's "style" as it is the nature of his books that discourages the layman. For instance, if the reader wishes to learn something about the Renaissance, he may be quite annoyed to encounter in the book of his choice a long discussion of the question whether there was a Renaissance at all, or, if there was one, whether it began earlier or later than historians have generally thought. While Pares did not discount the necessity for such writing and did not recommend that historians change their themes for the benefit of laymen, he did recognize that, from the average reader's viewpoint, the trouble with historians' writings is that "they are the wrong kind of books, written about the wrong kind of subject." [23]

If the gulf between historical specialists and laymen is wide, it is to some extent inevitable. It is one of the results of that specialization without which historianship would be unworthy of the name. There is no escaping the necessity for detailed research articles and monographs which will interest only a small audience even among historians. Without these writings the larger syntheses which many historians have the skill to construct and from which laymen can draw much profit would be impossible. George M. Trevelyan and Carl Becker have shown how the latter kind of writing can bring good history to the attention of average readers. And while but few Beckers or Trevelyans can be expected to appear during any generation, perhaps all historians would do well to ponder the admonition of amateur historian Theodore Roosevelt that "writings are useless unless they are read, and they cannot be read unless they are readable." [24] Happily, insofar as there is a problem in bringing new trends in historical thinking to the attention of teachers in the schools, publications of the American Historical Association's Service Center are accomplishing much toward supplying a solution.

Political history and institutional-origins history long dominated American historianship and gave to it a slant and to some extent a dullness from which it has never completely recovered. Herbert B. Adams, whom both J. Franklin Jameson and Woodrow Wilson thought superficial and showmanlike when they were graduate students of his at Johns Hopkins University,[25] indicated the emphasis at that institution. "The whole tenor of our researches at the J.H.U.," said Adams, "is to show the continuity of English institutions in the American," a keynote which had been struck for him by Edward A. Freeman.[26] For all its merit, this thesis minimized the influence of America's non-English strains upon development of institutions, and, more important, it neglected influences which sprang from the American environment.

It was because of this last factor, particularly, that Frederick J. Turner's frontier thesis, when announced in 1893, was welcomed as a breath of fresh air from the plains, mountains, and forests, and as something which might help purify a research atmosphere tending to grow stale. It was for a somewhat similar reason that Charles A. Beard's economic interpretation of the formation and adoption of the Constitution, announced twenty years later, was so well received. For however debatable may have been its central core, it was an American interpretation of American history, and, like the Turner thesis, it opened channels of research which seemed more significant and intellectually rewarding than investigations inspired by the Freeman-Adams philosophy.

But regardless of the philosophy or interpretation he may adopt, it seems only fair to say that the awarding of a doctorate to a prospective historian is an act of faith by his graduate department that he will rise to his responsibilities as a member of an honorable calling and will to some extent become a productive scholar. Only through the learned article here and the meticulous monograph there can the calling have any intellectual treasury to bequeath to posterity. Such writing requires much sacrifice. Boyd Shafer has reported that even prize volumes of the American Historical Association attract only a small audience,[27] and Johan Huizinga has shown that the problem of scholarly publication is not peculiar to the United States.[28]

THE HISTORIAN AS A REVIEWER

Included in the responsibilities of the historian is the task of reviewing books by his fellow craftsmen, as well as producing books of his own. Because of his experience in writing and seeing through the press a book from preface to index, and because he knows that reviewing is especially susceptible to subjectivity, the historian will, ideally at least, regard a review assignment as something worthy of his best efforts and the most scholarly integrity. At its best, a competent review in depth may be almost as important as the book itself.

Unfortunately, reviews sometimes fall short of the ideals with which the reviewer may be supposed to have approached his assignment. He may write, not a review of the book, but a short essay on the subject of the book, or he may summarize the book's contents and say nothing of the work's faults or merits. Equally disappointing is the review which calls attention to a few errors or debatable interpretations in the book but leaves the reader in doubt as to the reviewer's opinion of the work in its entirety. Occasionally a review may be strictly personal: the reviewer himself has written on the subject covered by the book and his appraisal of it is precisely in accordance with its agreement or disagreement with his own previous conclusions. Moreover, a reviewer may be tempted to reply, by indirection, to other reviews published before his own;[29] and in rare instances he may review the book in two separate publications and in the second review reply to repercussions caused by the first. Perhaps least serviceable of all reviews is the one that is so unduly flattering that it scarcely rises above the level of puffing.

The prototype of the modern highly critical review was Lord Macaulay's celebrated review of Robert Montgomery's poems, a review containing the words that "puffers . . . surely never played a more curious or a more difficult trick than when they passed Mr. Robert Montgomery off upon the world as a great poet." [30] And as one historian's caustic appraisal of another, Edward A. Freeman's comments on James A. Froude were in similar vein. Mr. Froude was, said Freeman, "the one writer of any consequence" on whose writings "any process of correction would be thrown away." "The evil," he said, was "inherent" and "inborn." "If history means truth, if it means fairness, if it means faithfully reporting what contemporary sources record, and drawing reasonable inferences from their statements, then," said Freeman, "Mr. Froude is no historian." [31]

If the reviewer sometimes forgets the canons that should guide him, it must also be said that an author sometimes proves so sensitive to any kind of criticism, however considerate and well founded, that he responds to it with a vehemence verging on the apoplectic. Where this is the case, or where a review is shocking, there is often an exchange of correspondence between author and reviewer which learned journals duly publish for the amusement if not the edification of the profession. Happily, most reviewers endeavor to be fair to the author and to say something about his book which will be helpful to persons who may wish to consult it.

A review may be unsatisfactory partly because of the limited space the reviewer is allowed, say four hundred to eight hundred words. While problems of space and expense are involved in the proposal, one cannot but hope that leading historical journals may sometime find it possible to carry only a few reviews per issue and make these full-length reviews of chapter size. A mere listing, with or without comments, of all other items received for review would be necessary if this plan were adopted. This concept of reviewing is, of course, not new. In 1912, for instance, Carl Becker advised that reviews be of two general types—one, a compact, bibliographical review or notice, the other, a detailed and critical review.[32]

That reviewing can be highly instructive has been shown in countless instances. In recent years it has been significantly demonstrated by the numerous reviews of Toynbee's *A Study of History* and by the learned and often brilliant and witty replies of the author to his critics. These qualities are probably nowhere better exemplified than in the reviews by Pieter Geyl and Sir Ernest Barker and the replies they elicited from Toynbee. It seems safe to say that these replies are some of the finest writing of our time—writing that is incisive but is at the same time softened by the author's gentleness and his sensitive appreciation for human personality.[33]

Important as reviewing is for the information of the historical fraternity and for maintenance of proper standards of scholarship, it sometimes has the unfortunate effect of discouraging publication. A sound but undistinguished scholar may hold off from publishing in the thought that his career would be unable to withstand adversely critical reviews, unmindful that only rarely are reviews uniformly devastating, and further, that readers are on the alert for the unfair review. With even more at stake careerwise than his less successful colleague, an eminent scholar sometimes assembles a vast quantity of material for a major work in his specialty, but postpones from year to year the actual writing so that he may not go into print until he has examined the last bit of evidence on his subject. The trouble with this view is, as Henri Pirenne has said, that all the materials of history will "never . . . be assembled;" hence, the historian is required only to "utilize all the data at his disposal at the moment." [34] Otherwise, our eminent scholar may allow himself to be badgered by imaginary reviewers into making preparation for his book—not the book itself—his magnum opus. Doing research and making and filing notes becomes his life-work, and his productive career ends with but little to show for it except files of notes which may be utterly worthless to surviving scholars.

Historians doubtless will agree with G. J. Renier that collecting documents and manuscripts is "preferable to the collecting of match-box labels or of company directorships," [35] since the former activity may enrich historical writing for years to come. Assembling notes for a book that never gets written, however, is a different matter. Such notes may be useless to posterity and have to be hauled away by a paid refuse collector.

Historians who are severely afflicted by "revieweritis" probably would do well to read the wise advice of Sir Charles Oman, who commented on the competent man who died "bookless . . . because he hated the idea of seeing his limitations revealed to the world by some captious critic." "The honest historian," said Sir Charles, "must not approach his life's work dominated by the pride which hates to acknowledge an occasional slip." His "guiding motive must be to strive for the increase of knowledge, not for the self-advertisement of the writer." [36] Perhaps a dash of Henry Adams's philosophy would also be beneficial to the patient. When informed of a critical review of some of the volumes of his History, Adams said that, while he did not welcome abuse, he was glad to know about the criticism, since it assured him that he had at least one unknown reader, a fact that he had previously doubted.[37]

THE AMERICAN CHARACTER AND AMERICAN HISTORY

IT MAY BE that the American character[1] is a "fictitious entity" in that the sum of its attributes does not represent a national type. These alleged attributes are numerous: conformity, uniformity, standardization, intolerance, friendliness, sincerity, hospitality, optimism, dynamism, enthusiasm, adaptability, self-reliance, and noncompliance. In addition, Americans are said to be given to generalization and over-simplification, and to suffer from a lack of privacy.[2] And British historian Richard Pares regarded a "tendency to law-breaking" among American business men as "the most disastrous legacy of the British Empire" to this class of citizens.[3] The foregoing is a formidable and, at points, a contradictory list of traits. No single group of Americans and no particular region of the country has all of them.[4]

THE CULT OF THE PRACTICAL

Not included in this list is a trait which has had an unusually potent influence in shaping the American outlook. This is an inordinate concern with practical values[5]—a concern that is apparent not only in economic affairs but also in intellectual matters as well. Max Weber thought there was a connection between this concern and religion, especially Protestantism.[6] In education the connection is more obvious. For while belief in education and its necessity in a democracy is shared by nearly all Americans, it often is conceived of as a means to a utilitarian end rather than as an end in itself— an enlargement of vision and an acquaintance with great minds, so that life, regardless of one's calling, will be richer and more meaningful.

This outlook was by no means an indigenous American development. The Anglo-Saxon element has always been dominant in America, and if there was ever a civilization whose leaders thought in materialistic terms—in terms of pounds, shillings, and pence—it was the civilization of seventeenth- and eighteenth-century England, from which American civilization drew most heavily. This factor probably deserves more study than it has hitherto received by specialists on the American Revolution and its background.

It is ironic and at the same time a happy circumstance that the American patron saint of the practical should also have been one of the most broadly educated men of his time and deeply appreciative of literature, languages, and the arts. For if Benjamin Franklin is best remembered for the wisdom of *Poor Richard*— "Keep thy shop, and thy shop will keep thee," or, "Now that I have a sheep and a cow, every body bids me good morrow"—he was nevertheless one of the few Americans of his time who felt at home with the savants of the Old World. And one may suppose that Franklin, if now living, would deplore the fact that the humanities and the social sciences suffer great hurts in competition with the natural sciences and engineering.

THE CULT OF BIGNESS

Closely related to our concern with the practical is the cult of bigness. This cult springs from the enormous territorial extent of America, its relatively large population, and the mammoth undertakings launched for its development. Because of a prevalent quantitative thinking, the student who writes a master's essay or a doctoral dissertation needs to be prepared for an almost complete lack of curiosity about his thesis among his non-academic acquaintances, except for one almost unfailing question: How many pages has it? The fact that this question is so common (and it is by no means uncommon on campuses of large universities) is a reflection of a prominent trait in the American character.

From virtually the beginnings of our history, quantitative thinking has been a controlling factor in America. Our colonial establishments, and then our states and nation, expanded prodigiously; "manifest destiny" carried Americans and their way of life to the far reaches of our present-day boundaries. But the spirit of "manifest destiny," although the term was not coined until 1845,[7] inspired the nation because it had already inspired the individual. The farmer starting with forty acres could not be content until he had acquired the adjoining south forty, and then the two additional forty's to give him a quarter-section. And the more ambitious farmer would push on toward acquisition of a section (640 acres) or more. The farmer thus exemplified the doctrine of "manifest destiny" on a one-man scale long before it became a national expansionist slogan.

Perhaps to a greater extent than is generally realized, quantitative thinking has also helped shape popular attitudes toward the three branches of the Federal Government. In this instance, the thinking is in terms of an ascending scale of power per man, not in terms of mere numbers. Thus, assuming that the three branches are equally powerful, the Congress, the Supreme Court, and the Presidency are in an ascending scale of power per man. Congress is a powerful body, but its power is wielded by 537 men, and the prestige of an individual member, being scaled to his power, is relatively small. And the Senate is a more prestigious body than the House, because the Senate's power is exercised by 100 persons, whereas the House's power is exercised by 437. No amount of constitutional and historical argument, however sound, by Speaker McCormack and others, is likely to equalize the two houses in popular prestige, for the simple reason that the Senate's power per member is over four times that of the House. Likewise, the Supreme Court enjoys its tremendous prestige not only because it interprets the laws and the Constitution, but also because this far-reaching power is exercised by only nine men. A supreme Court Justice therefore has some sixty times the power of a member of Congress. At the peak of this power pyramid stands the Presidency, for here one man controls the vast power of the executive branch of the Government. Basically, it is the power vested in this one-man office, and not the physical appearance of the President, however attractive, which evokes the wide range of favorable emotions toward him and causes multitudes to wish to see him and shake his hand. By contrast, only a mild interest may be evoked by the presence of a Supreme Court Justice and little or no interest at all by the presence of a Congressman.

THE CULT OF INDIVIDUALISM

This concept of power per man is a phase of a larger concept of individualism. Actually, much that has been written about the role of the "sturdy individual" in American history will not bear close scrutiny. There always have been sturdy Americans, but the notion that sturdy individualism as a way of life was voluntarily and joyously assumed by them, even when this meant inconvenience and torturous drudgery, is pure myth. For despite the nostalgia said to be inspired by stories of the self-sufficient farm life of earlier days, there is no evidence that farmers did not abandon this Arcadian existence at the first opportunity. Excepting some small groups, such as the Amish of Lancaster County, Pennsylvania, American farmers have taken to improved agricultural implements and automotive vehicles with the greatest alacrity. Nor have farm women shown any particular zeal for continuing the use of washboards, hand-churns, and wood-burning kitchen stoves in an age of electricity and mechanical appliances. Countless farm families have also become reconciled with the greatest of ease to having the plumbing located indoors. In all this, rural Americans have abided by a rule of personal efficiency which has been defined as the mental and physical ability of finding the easiest, the best, and the quickest way to the desirable things of life.

Nor does rural democracy, upon examination, fare much better than rural individualism. Both derived more from physical environment than from philosophical speculation. With his usual incisiveness and discernment, George Macaulay Trevelyan has said that lack of good and speedy means of communication and transportation in medieval England had much more to do with the rise of democracy in that country than did Magna Carta. The hard fact that a king or his agents could not bring continuous and consistent authority to bear in remote rural areas and villages left Englishmen an opportunity to go much their own way.[8] Similarly, because their country was large, settlements sparse, and means of communication and transportation inadequate rural Americans developed individual liberty and concepts of self-reliance to an unusual degree. If one may be permitted to criticize his betters, however, it is easy to make the mistake, as did Frederick J. Turner, of equating these principles too largely with democracy. Whether exercised on the frontier or in the most sophisticated eastern metropolis, individual freedom could and often did take the form of conduct inimical to social progress and the general welfare. Much American economic, social, and constitutional history is concerned with the conflict between these individual and social forces and with efforts to reconcile them. Abraham Lincoln, perhaps despairing of ever seeing Americans become completely social beings, was quoted as having said that "all there is to honest statesmanship is controlling and directing individual meannesses for the public good." [9] Perhaps Lincoln would have agreed that if the individual is the salient unit in the American political society, then only through a process of "institutionalized individualism" [10] is there hope for securing justice for all Americans, individually and collectively.

THE CULT OF DEMOCRATIC ACCOMMODATION

As for the respective roles of the individual and society in the United States, it may be offered as some justification of our democracy that it has measurably succeeded in reconciling individual and group aspirations. In the process of reaching this adjustment, however, there has been a steady trend toward circumscribing individual in favor of collective action, and some students have lamented the passing of the free individual to make way for welfarism. Of course, no man has ever been free in any absolute sense. The catchy dictum of Jean Jacques Rousseau that "Man is born free, and yet we see him everywhere in chains," [11] was good revolutionary propaganda in late eighteenth-century France, but was false history. The very seasons, together with droughts, floods, storms, and other natural disasters have always held man in leading-strings, and he has had to adjust himself to these restraints or perish. Americans early discovered that certain social necessities might better be met by collective than by individual action. Construction and maintenance of roads and bridges, handling of the mail, providing educational opportunities for youth, making provision for the indigent, and maintaining a defense system all were examples of necessary activities that might possibly have been performed by individuals but could be performed better and more economically by government.

Much of our history has been a story of a developing social conscience, of a movement away from the self-centered, antisocial individualism of earlier days, toward a concept of a social, economic, and political order having the general welfare as its goal. During the past half-century, the area of collective action has expanded and we have moved toward what Carl Becker called "Social Democracy."

Inasmuch as one of the grand objects of the Constitution of 1787 was to "promote the general welfare," and providing for the "general welfare" was one of the purposes of the taxing power assigned Congress by the Constitution, it seems strange that later so much effort should have been made to deny this power to the Federal Government and to make promotion of the general welfare appear as a strange and alien doctrine. Paradoxically, however, certain of the forces that have consistently opposed the march towards the welfare state, have done much to accelerate it. Thus, the reasoning back of the great philanthropies was that certain individuals, because of their gifts for money-making, should utilize society to build fortunes and then give back to society a portion of their accumulations. It was said that in this way philanthropists conferred upon society benefits that society, left to its own awkward devices, would never confer upon itself. Many rich men unwittingly followed the advice given by socialist George Bernard Shaw in his *Socialism for Millionaires* that philanthropists should give to society, not what it wants, but what it ought to want and does not.[12] What philanthropists apparently did not see was that if it was proper for them to take from society money in the form of profits and use a part of these to build institutions of social usefulness, it obviously would be more proper still for organized government to take from society money in the form of general and equitably assessed taxes and, with funds thus raised, build and maintain these institutions.

Indeed, when the government nowadays siphons off funds from taxpayers to support various forms of social welfare, it is acting upon the philosophy underlying the creation of tax-exempt foundations that support projects of social and cultural value. Well before the "New Deal" of Franklin Roosevelt's administration, there were in nearly all parts of the country foundation-supported libraries, universities, hospitals, museums, and research institutions which served as living symbols of how the general welfare might be promoted by fiscal sources not necessarily related immediately to the geographical areas benefited. It is really little wonder that we have had in this country a steady drift toward the welfare, or, as the late Roscoe Pound chose to call it, the "service" state.[13]

Free enterprise, through welfare capitalism in the form of retirement plans, group insurance, and other fringe benefits for employees, has significantly supplemented the drive toward the welfare state that private philanthropy has done so much to promote. For welfare capitalism, like philanthropy, recognizes economic and social needs which must be met at a level other than that of the individual. The influence of welfare capitalism upon government in the matter of health insurance and other fringe benefits for Federal employees seems obvious. And more than one citizen has wondered why, if federally subsidized health insurance is proper and is financially feasible for Government employees, similar insurance, financed through the Social Security system, would not be appropriate for all citizens whose employment comes under that system. With enactment in 1965 of a "Medicare Bill" for the aged, Congress took a long step toward acceptance of this point of view.

THE CULT OF PROGRESS

But cults of the practical, of bigness, of individualism, and of democratic accommodation all gained vogue in America because they seemed to be media for individual and social advancement. The concept of advancement itself, however, was not peculiar to America. From the Enlightenment of the eighteenth century through World War I, belief in "progress" was widespread in the Western world, and in England in the early part of the twentieth century it formed the philosophical basis for *The Cambridge Modern History*. British historian Edward H. Carr has observed that such a belief is essential to society, inasmuch as each generation is required to make sacrifices for the generations to come. If men disbelieved in progress and felt that society was merely a vehicle spinning its wheels in loose sand, plans for the future would seem futile.[14]

Progress sometimes requires change, and for this reason it may be slow. As Morris R. Cohen has said, "Inertia is the first law of history, as it is of physics." [15] Even in the Declaration of Independence, American Revolutionary statesmen said that men are disposed to tolerate governmental injustice as long as possible rather than make a change. And their written Constitution of 1787 might seem to suggest an American predisposition against change.

But independence was declared, and one of the great political changes of modern times was thereby consummated; and the Constitution, supposedly "fixed" because written, was to prove remarkably flexible through amendment and judicial interpretation. American society has always been dynamic, and a doctrine of constitutional statics has never harmonized with its requirements.

James Schouler once said that "the only clear law of history is that of motion incessantly onward." [16] But mere motion does not imply progress. Nor do improved means to an end. As H. D. Thoreau commented, the railroad improved means of travel from Concord to Boston and New York without improving those two cities.[17] Nevertheless, American history suggests that resistance to change may produce imbalances that can be corrected only by drastic, even dangerous, measures. It was an imbalance in American society and economy which produced the "New Deal" and the "Fair Deal"; and many citizens, including President Franklin D. Roosevelt,[18] were convinced that the corrective measures of the 1930's saved the nation from revolution. That there are imbalances in the nation still—especially in matters of education, health, and employment—seems evident; and it may be supposed that these problems will continue to perplex politicians and statesmen for many years to come.

To Harvard economist John K. Galbraith, social balance is achieved when there is a "satisfactory relationship" between privately and publicly produced goods and services. And with perhaps too much faith in the efficacy of educational, recreational, and other public services to transform society, Galbraith sees in an expansion of these services the possibility of virtually eliminating poverty itself. From his viewpoint, the problem of establishing social balance is primarily one for government at the state and local levels, and the funds required for the necessary services may be had by imposing, or increasing, sales taxes. Important as it is, however, to have a strong program of public services at the local level, and cogent as are the arguments for a sales tax to finance them, it may well be doubted whether the major problems of American social imbalance can be met by these expedients.[19] These problems are national in their scope and implications, and justice in dealing with them requires uniformity of policy. Our history indicates that uniformity of policy is unlikely to be had except through federal action.

But if change has at times meant progress, it has at other times meant the opposite. Change in manufacturing may derive largely from a desire to sell the maximum number of units in the minimum amount of time. The resultant pressure to sell has led to manufacture of appliances, machines, and commodities with built-in obsolescence. If this were not so, runs the argument, then less employment would be required to meet consumer demand and the entire economy would lag.

Certain aspects of presentism in historical writing suggest that in the intellectual as well as in the material world, change may be confused with progress. A change in historical interpretation sometimes comes about, not because of any significant new factual findings, but because of changed economic, social, or political conditions. Thus, we have a "New Deal," and soon much American history is rewritten in terms of the new order. Or the Supreme Court announces new decisions on race relations, and soon we have a flood of books and articles reflecting the changed viewpoint and re-examining the story of slavery, the Civil War, and Reconstruction. On the basis of past performances by American historians in responding to presentist influences, it may be conjectured that the next important change in historianship in this country will be a transfer of interest from national, state, and local history to the international scene. In some quarters, nationalism has already become anathema, and Arnold J. Toynbee, whose writings have enjoyed unusual popularity in the United States, sees the creation of new national states as a grave sin.* In any event, a new generation is likely to find new themes and new approaches, and the interpretations of our own day may seem to historians of tomorrow naive and unimaginative.

Of one thing we may be fairly certain: if, in the larger context of our history, Americans, including historians, have sometimes mistaken motion and change for progress, there can be no denying that the American people have achieved progress in many segments of their life. We are, for instance, better clothed, fed, and housed than ever before, and we have opened or are rapidly opening avenues of education to all capable youth willing to pursue them. Unfortunately, making men more comfortable and knowledgeable may not make them more just or moral, and it is thus in the spir-

* See above, p. 56.

itual realm that the American cult of progress is most vulnerable and has proved most disappointing.

THE CULT OF INVINCIBILITY

Complementing the foregoing cults, there has been until recently an American national self-confidence so massive as to constitute a cult of invincibility. For although this country was invaded and suffered some humiliation during the Revolutionary War and the War of 1812, Americans could boast that they had never lost a war. This pattern of victory had a profound effect upon American foreign-policy outlook. Not a belligerent people but an assured and confident people, Americans felt that wars were to be fought only as a last resort and when fought were to be won. Any other outcome was unthinkable. Protected by two oceans and with no hostile or powerful neighbors on the north or south, Americans entered no war after 1815 in which there was any serious danger of invasion or loss of territory.

But the Korean War, the oddest contest in which this nation has ever engaged, changed American military and foreign-policy conceptions. Officially a UN war against North Korean Communist aggressors aided by Red Chinese, the struggle was essentially an American war against these forces. And although in two world wars America's freedom of action had been somewhat circumscribed by the interest of partners, it was in the Korean War particularly that Americans learned that they might have to compromise their judgment on matters of vital interest to the United States. For whether or not an all-out war against Chinese Reds—a necessary action if the UN intended to control North Korea—would have led to Russian intervention and a third world war, the fact is that the all-out effort was not made and the issue was finally settled by UN acceptance of a Korean dividing line which was largely the line dividing the country before the war. It was said with truth that the war had demonstrated that the UN could and would resist aggressors. In that sense the war was a UN victory. But the equivocal settlement seemed actually to be a defeat for the UN and for its chief defender, the United States. And this had resulted, not from American inability to carry the war to a victorious conclusion, but from UN counsels, acquiesced in by Washington, that the issue was not worth risking a third world war.

For these reasons, countless Americans were left with a feeling of frustration and with an uneasy intimation, now experienced for the first time in their lives, that their country did not control its own destiny—that it was so involved in the fate of other nations that it might be obliged to go to war, refrain from war, or allow a war to end in stalemate because its partners so advised.[20] And thermonuclear weapons, by reducing the old-fashioned American military virtues of bravery, courage, and inventiveness to the vanishing point, have served to intensify Americans' sense of frustration. As Robert L. Heilbroner has said, the American people, within a period of thirty years, have had to change their viewpoint from one of national security to one of "defensive insecurity." [21] Today, no thoughtful American would say that his country is invincible. He might say with plausibility that any country that destroyed America would itself be destroyed by her. But this attitude is a far cry from the cult of invincibility which dominated our thinking for a century and a half—the belief that we could win any war we entered and emerge without mortal wounds. In retrospect, it seems clear that the American cult of invincibility was started toward the limbo when the first successful nuclear chain reaction was achieved on the campus of the University of Chicago in 1942 during World War II.

AMERICA IN THE PATTERN OF WESTERN CULTURE

Whatever her cults, America derived from and has never ceased to be a part of the civilization of the West. It has also been the good fortune of the United States and its people that while they could retain their Western connections they could at the same time deviate from Western cultural patterns to suit their environmental needs and their concepts of national destiny. Twice during our century, America has entwined her destiny with that of the Western world and the very survival of that world has depended to a large extent upon American policy and action. For America has long since come to see that whatever uniqueness she may possess is a uniqueness within a matrix of a larger culture.

The tides of modern Western philosophy affect our shores quite as much as those of Europe. Thus, when Oswald Spengler announced that Western civilization was in decline,[22] and Arnold J. Toynbee declared that this civilization had a chance but not too strong a chance for survival,[23] they spoke to Americans quite as much as to Englishmen and Europeans. Likewise did anthropologist Alfred L. Kroeber, who suggested more encouragingly that Western civilization was in a process of "reconstituting" itself, much as it did during the era of the Renaissance and the Reformation.[24] And Bertrand Russell, who certainly has been restrained in his praise of Western culture, has acknowledged four major advances made by it: the near elimination of poverty, reduction of illness and death rates, wide diffusion of education, and a new harmonization of freedom and order.[25]

At the same time, Russell has been profoundly disturbed by the recent subordination of man's better to his baser nature, and by the rise of abnormality and irrationality to the level of respectability. With Russell's view, Lewis Mumford is in agreement. Likening the good and bad in man to Shakespeare's Prospero and Caliban in *The Tempest,* Mumford concludes sadly that we "live under the sign of Caliban." Moreover, finding parallels in Sigmund Freud's conceptions of the id (the primitive self), the ego (the conventional self), and the superego (the censorious self), Mumford sees the disintegration of the superego—the self that inhibits and represses and raises questions as to the justice or morality of a given action— and the ascendancy of the id, or the self of unrestrained and primitive urges. This, he says, has resulted from an abuse of Freud's teaching that certain illnesses originate in excessive repression by the superego, and from the false conclusion that these illnesses may be avoided by subordinating the superego to the id.[26]

Over a century ago, Auguste Comte proposed a regeneration of society through "positivism," a process which presumably would have corrected tendencies toward those traits in man so much deplored by Russell and Mumford in our own day. Acting outside a Christian context, Comte aimed "to systematize the art of social life." Taking as its motto, "Love, Order, Progress," positivism sought to revitalize society, a task which Comte said it could perform better than could the Church. But he insisted that positivism was not atheism, materialism, fatalism, or optimism, but a system in which heart would be supreme over intellect, and reason subordinate to feeling.

Comte made his appeal chiefly to women, whom he regarded as "the original source of all moral influence," and to the working classes. This he did because these two groups had not had their "good sense" impaired "by our vicious system of education" and because their "generous sympathies" could "develop themselves freely." And since they had little influence in political government, women and workers were more likely than others to appreciate moral government.

Positivism, as Comte conceived it, was a "religion of Humanity" which had as its end a universal society. The latter's proposed "Permanent Council" and certain other administrative features were strongly prophetic of the later League of Nations and United Nations.[27]

Though thinking chiefly in terms of industrial civilization and its future, University of Chicago economist John U. Nef arrived at views strikingly similar to those of scholars who have approached a study of modern civilization from a broader philosophical viewpoint. Nef sees the industrial civilization of the future depending less upon scientific and technical skill and more upon human attributes heretofore regarded as "useless" in an economic sense. Thus, the new dominant "quantitative economy" would come under the direction of an "economy of delight, in the service of the good. . . ." And like Mumford and Toynbee and many other thoughtful religious persons, Nef sees in the "love and charity" as taught by Christ the road to salvation for modern man and his civilization.[28]

Logician Karl R. Popper regards as the crucial question of our times whether we are to have an "open society" of political and spiritual freedom or a "closed society" of centralization and regimentation.[29] And thinking along somewhat similar lines, John Gardner, President of the Carnegie Corporation of New York and of the Carnegie Foundation for the Advancement of Teaching,* sees in hospitality toward innovation and tolerance for dissent the possibility of achieving a society that will be "ever-renewing." [30]

That these various theories have relevance for American history seems obvious. May it not be said, for instance, that one phase of American civilization—an era of more or less unrestrained free enterprise and maldistribution of products of industry—ended with the year 1933 and that a new phase was then inaugurated? And yet the "New Deal" was no social and economic cataclysm and did not mark a complete break with the past. It was rather, to use

* Now (1966) Secretary of Health, Education, and Welfare.

the word that Kroeber has given us, a "reconstituting" of American society; and the process was informed and guided by a will to give concepts of human decency and justice a wider application than they had ever enjoyed before in the United States.

But American social advances since 1933, significant as they have been, do not in themselves assure that the "open society" will permanently triumph in this country. Serious choices remain to be made, and a wrong turning could lead us into a blind alley from which there could be no retreat. As we have noted, the late Carl Becker, writing in the midst of World War II, expressed the opinion that the United States would have to choose between fascism, communism, socialism, and social democracy; and while his personal preference was social democracy, Becker warned that fascism would be our lot unless we exercised great care.[31] It was the opinion of Charles A. Beard that the entire world was moving toward a collectivist democracy.[32]

If it is granted that the trend of our times in America is toward the welfare, or service state[33] (Becker's social democracy), with government doing more and more for the people and collecting more and more taxes to finance the operation, a query seems inescapable: Can we continue on this road without finally having to surrender to government our freedom of choice in matters hitherto never entrusted to public authority? This question is pertinent because of what happened in Germany and Italy between the two world wars and because of what has happened in Russia and other Communist areas of the world. The "charismatic chief" of the type that made an appearance in Italy[34] and Germany during the 1930's, and who seemed to some of his followers to be supernatural, has never gained a hold in America—not quite. But throughout our national history we have had leaders who showed marked signs of the "charismatic," and we shall be lucky if we do not have others.

Karl Jaspers has suggested that a people can become "irrational" and "freely resolve to have no more freedom." [35] And David M. Potter believes that "no one has ever proved that humanity really prefers freedom to security. . . ." [36] Fortunately, people in American have not had to choose between freedom and security. Here they have assumed, and their experience has confirmed the assumption, that while concepts of freedom and security are relative, the one cannot be had without the other. This national conviction affords hope that continuing ways will be found to promote the general welfare without sacrificing the "open society" of individual freedom and initiative.

INTERPRETING AMERICAN HISTORY

In light of the foregoing discussion in this chapter it may be asked whether there has been anything unique about American history and whether there has been any unifying principle in its unfolding. For if it is true, as Lincoln said, that we cannot escape history, neither can we escape a desire to understand it. In seeking this understanding, American writings often prove unrewarding. Many Americans have written on the philosophy of history, but relatively few have attempted to formulate interpretations of American history as distinct from general history. Thus, Brooks Adams, Henry Adams, F. J. Teggart, E. P. Cheyney, Shailer Mathews, and Edwin R. A. Seligman, among others, directed their philosophical writings toward an understanding of American history only insofar as American history served to explain history generally.

Of the two American historians, Charles A. Beard and Frederick J. Turner, who may be said to have established "schools" of American history, only Turner was concerned primarily with American history. Beard, known as the founder of the economic interpretation of American history, by no means limited his philosophical excursions to American history. What he said about causation, relativism, presentism, and history as thought and as an act of faith, was universal, not national or regional in its application.[37] And Carl Becker, one of the most fertile minds in the annals of American historiography, likewise was concerned with historical conceptions of a general character.

Some American scholars have interpreted phases of American history rather than its totality; however, these phases have relevance for more than a single specialty. Roscoe Pound and James W. Hurst, in interpreting American legal history, have made helpful suggestions for a better understanding of economic and social history.[38] Moreover, it has been shown that the value of legal history as a synthesizing factor in general history has not been sufficiently recognized by the historical fraternity. As an example of what this field may hold for the historian, it may be noted that the *Commentaries on the Laws of England,* by Sir William Blackstone, "provided a major synthesis of ideas drawn from history, law, and the social sciences." [39]

Dominant or synthesizing themes in American intellectual and social history have been sought by several scholars, among whom may be mentioned Dixon R. Fox, John Higham, and Rowland Berthoff, Joseph Dorfman has shown how rewarding for our general history can be an exploration of American economic thought from the colonial era into our own times.[40]

The views widely accepted in the historical profession that historians must be concerned with the individual and the unique, that their job is primarily to relate what happened, and that history is not a science and has no laws—all have served to leave the field of generalization and interpretation to others, mainly to philosophers and sociologists. The latter scholars appreciate history as "essentially a descriptive science" which provides accurate data that sociologists may interpret and "resolve . . . into laws of cause and effect." [41] Wilhelm Dilthey, while agreeing with this judgment of history, doubted that sociologists would be able to perform the tasks of analysis and interpretation which historians had rejected.[42]

Inasmuch as American history is a subject to which American youths are exposed from elementary school through college, it may seem ironical that historians should not have had more influence than they have had upon the Nation's cultural and intellectual growth. The pattern of American cultural concepts is a product of many minds; and to the extent that historians have contributed to the pattern's formation, this often has been achieved by giving currency to the conclusions of non-historians rather than by advancing their own. True, historians such as Beard, Becker, and Robinson did much to free history from the limitations of German historiography and make it more nearly a life-discipline. But Oliver Wendell Holmes, Roscoe Pound, and James W. Hurst, in relating law to social change; Vernon L. Parrington, in formulating an economic approach to the study of American literature; John Dewey, in showing the pragmatic bases for social thinking; and the University of Chicago psychologists and political scientists, in conceiving of democracy not merely as a form of government but also as "a mode of associated living" with numerous "areas of shared concern," have done most to shape the American *Weltanschauung.*[43]

As for a unifying theme in American history, it may be said that from the colonial era forward the dominant factor in the American story has been a generally held conception of the rights of man. Men came to these shores in quest of an order in which they might have a larger degree of dignity, freedom, and security than they had known before. Could they have been content without this, there would have been little point in their coming to America.

This hope of realizing an enlargement of human rights has been an even more important feature of American history since the colonial era than during that time. The ideal is implicit in the liberalization of the franchise as it evolved from religious and property qualifications to general manhood suffrage and finally to universal suffrage for men and women alike. It is also implicit in our educational history, from the restricted opportunities available in pauper, charity, and tuition schools to the free, tax-supported schools of our own day. Recent steps toward bringing college and graduate-school education within the reach of all capable and aspiring youth are a further refinement of the notion that education is a basic human right and essential to the proper functioning of the citizen in organized society.

A century ago, Englishman Henry Thomas Buckle noted that knowledge in Germany was deep and abundant but was enjoyed by only a small percentage of the people, whereas in America it was less profound and abundant but was widely diffused among the people.[44] The "masscult" of our own day has at least the merit of universal education, beginnings of which Buckle appreciated.

The human-rights influence can likewise be traced in the history of American labor-management relations and in general labor legislation. Even in a day of little or no labor regulation, such evils as long hours, low wages, and child labor did not escape protesting voices. Conditions were gradually improved: the twelve-hour day gave way to the ten, and the ten to the eight; wages were raised in terms of buying power; child labor was abolished or strictly controlled; and group insurance and a host of other fringe benefits were made available to workers. There has also developed in America, especially since 1933, the notion of a minimum standard of living to which every human being is entitled. The country has steadily moved forward toward this goal for all its citizens.

In other major areas of our history also, a concept of human rights has been determinative. In our diplomacy, for example, there has been much moralizing[45] and most of our wars have been conceived of as struggles for human rights, however much this theory has been based in some instances upon a tortured logic.

No theory of history is without exceptions, and the human-rights interpretation of American history finds its two major flaws in United States Indian policy and in public and private racial policy and practice. While mistreatment of Indians and Negroes has never gone without some condemnation by whites, it has been with respect to these two social groups that Americans have been slowest in putting their idealistic professions of human rights into practice. Deplorable as the tardiness of advance has been, however, it is significant that Indians and Negroes have gradually—and in recent years, rapidly—advanced toward the goal of human rights enjoyed by other American citizens.

As previously suggested, the entire complex of measures commonly subsumed under the term of "New Deal" was designed mainly to help Americans realize the human potential which a majority of the people had come to believe was theirs as of right. Students of the law have noted that the law has been amenable to social and intellectual change.[46] Theoretically, courts might have declared much recent wage-and-hour and other labor legislation void. In earlier days judges were able to find in the Constitution reasons for such adverse action. In more recent years, however, much legislation favorable to labor has been sustained by courts, not because of Constitutional change but because of popular intellectual and social change.

Social mobility, both as to freedom of movement by individuals and groups about the country, and the movement of individuals up and down the socio-economic ladder,[47] is another phase of the larger human-rights concept that we are examining. For unless men and women have the right to go to whatever state, city, or town they think most advantageous to themselves,[48] and unless avenues of occupational and professional advancement are open to all on a fair and equal competitive basis, they will enjoy something less than what human beings in an "open society" have a right to expect.

That establishing equality of human rights does not solve all social and economic problems is evident; and that it even brings some evils in its train must be equally obvious. But the wrongs that result from abuse of the human-rights concept, such, for instance, as infliction of selfish or vicious propaganda upon the reading masses whose reading and reasoning powers have developed unequally, are more than counterbalanced by the strengths of an open society of liberty and equality. Any substitute for this society is unthinkable to the average American, and there is every reason to suppose that American history will continue to reflect the aspirations of a people moving steadily toward an order of economic and social justice.

It has been suggested that our social concepts must be given to the world—that complementing the victory of the three R's over illiteracy, America must now conquer poverty with the three E's. Our goal, we are told, must be "Everything for and with Everybody Everywhere," climaxed by a "fourth E of Excellence by Everybody in Everything through Enterprising and Education." To reach this goal, runs the theory, we must have a plan of "codevelopment" with underdeveloped countries, and a program of "humanation or full participation of all individuals in the productive process." [49]

While this idealistic goal may be impossible of complete attainment, may it not be that the American doctrine of human rights will reach fruition only when its benefits are universally diffused? And may not this be the larger meaning of American history?

NOTES

INTRODUCTION

1. Ibn Khaldûn, *The Muqaddimah: An Introduction to History,* trans. Franz Rosenthal (3 vols.; New York: Pantheon Books, for Bollingen Foundation, 1958), I, 15. The word "different" in parentheses before the word "approaches" in the text was supplied by the translator.

2. See Reinhold Niebuhr, *Christian Realism and Political Problems* (New York: Scribner's Sons, 1953), p. 83, citing Robert MacIver's view on multiple causation in history, such as the geographic, climatic, psychological, and others.

3. Georg Wilhelm Friedrich Hegel, *The Philosophy of History* (Great Books of the Western World, ed. Robert M. Hutchins, Vol. 46; Chicago: Encyclopaedia Britannica, Inc., 1952), p. 154.

4. Henry Thomas Buckle, *History of Civilization in England* (2nd ed., 2 vols.; New York: D. Appleton and Company, 1876).

5. Edward P. Cheyney, "Law in History," *American Historical Review,* XXIX (Jan., 1924), 231-48. For a recent formulation of historical "laws," see Ernest Cuneo, *Science and History* (New York: Duell, Sloan and Pearce, 1963).

6. John Maynard Keynes, *A Treatise on Probability* (London: Macmillan Company, 1929), p. 407.

7. Cf. *Saturday Review,* Dec. 8, 1962, p. 65.

CHAPTER I

1. Henri Bergson, *The Creative Mind,* trans. Mabelle L. Andison (New York: Philosophical Library, 1946), p. 9.

2. G. J. Renier, *History: Its Purposes and Methods* (Boston: Beacon Press, 1950), pp. 49-50.

3. Shailer Mathews, *The Spiritual Interpretation of History* (Cambridge: Harvard University Press, 1916), p. 31.

4. Frederick J. Teggart, "Causation in Historical Events," *Journal of the History of Ideas,* III (Jan., 1942), 3.

5. Ernst Bernheim, *Lehrbuch der Historischen Methode und der Geschichtsphilosophie, Mit Nachweis der wichtigsten Quellen und Hilfsmittel zum Studium der Geschichte* (2 vols.; New York: Burt Franklin, 1960 [published originally, 1889]), I, 10.

6. Cf. Carl L. Becker, *The Heavenly City of the Eighteenth-Century Philosophers* (New Haven: Yale University Press, 1932), p. 119.

7. Karl R. Popper, *The Open Society and Its Enemies* (Princeton: Princeton University Press, 1950), p. 393. Paul Weiss has said: "The present is bounded off from the past, and terminates in the future, to constitute a single, limited ongoing historic unit" (*History: Written and Lived* [Carbondale, Ill.: Southern Illinois University Press, 1962], p. 145).

8. Cf. W. Stull Holt, "The Idea of Scientific History in America," *Journal of the History of Ideas,* I (July, 1940), 352-62.

9. *The Complete Writings of Thucydides: The Peloponnesian War,* unabridged Crawley trans., with Intro. by Joseph Gavorse (New York: Random House, 1934), pp. 14-15.

10. *The Complete Works of Tactitus,* trans. Alfred John Church and William Jackson Brodribb (New York: Random House, 1942).

11. Ordericus Vitalis, *The Ecclesiastical History of England and Normandy,* trans. Thomas Forester, with notes; Intro. by Guizot (4 vols.; London: Henry G. Bohn, 1853-56), II, 121-22.

12. R. W. Church, *St. Anselm* (new ed.; London: Macmillan and Company, 1881), p. 112.

13. Cf. Theodore Clarke Smith, "The Writing of American History in America, from 1884 to 1934," *American Historical Review,* XL (April, 1935), 440.

14. Charles H. Haskins, *The Normans in European History* (Boston: Houghton Mifflin, 1915), p. 180. See also p. 183.

15. *Op. cit.,* I, 3.

16. Arnold J. Toynbee, *A Study of History* (12 vols.; London: Oxford University Press, 1934-61), III, 332.

17. Cf. *An Arab Philosophy of History: Selections from the Prolegomena of Ibn Khaldûn of Tunis (1332–1406),* trans. Charles Issawi (London: John Murray, 1950), pp. 27-29, *et passim.* Also Ibn Khaldûn, *The Muqaddimah: An Introduction to History,* Vol. I.

18. James Westfall Thompson, with Bernard J. Holm, *A History of Historical Writing* (2 vols.; New York: Macmillan Company, 1942), II, 93-94. The scientific character of the historical writings of Niccolo Machiavelli (1469–1527) and Francesco Guicciardini (1482–

1540) is discussed by John Addington Symonds in *Renaissance in Italy* (2 vols.; New York: The Modern Library, 1935), I, 152-56; and II, 419-20. Perhaps the most celebrated of the European Renaissance critics was Italian Lorenzo Valla (1406?-1457) who won fame for proving the falsity of the long-accepted Donation of Constantine. Cf. Eduard Fueter, *Geschichte der Neuren Historiographie* (München und Berlin: R. Oldenbourg, 1911), p. 112.

19. R. G. Collingwood, *The Philosophy of History* ([London]: G. Bell and Sons, Ltd., for the Historical Association, 1930), p. 6. In agreement with Collingwood is H. P. Adams, *The Life and Writings of Giambattista Vico* (London: George Allen and Unwin, Ltd., 1935), p. 212, and pp. 207-22 *passim*.

20. Benedetto Croce, *History as the Story of Liberty*, trans. Sylvia Sprigge (New York: W. W. Norton, 1941), pp. 71-72.

21. *The Cambridge Modern History* (12 vols.; New York: Macmillan Company, 1934 [published originally, 1902-10]), XII, 818-19. See also G. P. Gooch, *History and Historians in the Nineteenth Century* (3rd impr.; New York: Longmans, Green and Company, 1920), p. 14.

22. Gooch, *op. cit.*, p. 825.

23. Ferdinand Schevill, *Six Historians* (Chicago: University of Chicago Press, 1956), pp. 125-55; also, Harold Temperley, *Selected Essays of J. B. Bury* (Cambridge: At the University Press, 1930), pp. 10, 19.

24. Benedetto Croce has written of "such a minor and philosophically indifferent and inexpert mind as that of Leopold von Ranke" (*op. cit.*, p. 78).

25. Charles A. Beard, "That Noble Dream," *American Historical Review*, XLI (Oct., 1935), 74-87. Johann Gottfried von Herter (1744-1803) who recognized that the only attainable objectivity is "relative objectivity," said that he wrote history only "as it appears to me, as I come to know it." See F. M. Barnard, "Herter's Treatment of Causation and Continuity in History," *Journal of the History of Ideas*, XXIV (April-June, 1963), 197-212, especially 198-99. A similar view was advanced by C. V. Langlois and C. Seignobos in *Introduction to the Study of History* (trans. G. G. Berry [New York: Henry Holt, 1892], p. 217): "From the very nature of its materials history is necessarily a subjective science."

26. Carl Becker, "Everyman His Own Historian," *American Historical Review*, XXXVII (Jan., 1932), 221-36. The quotation is from p. 233.

27. Charles Kendall Adams, "Recent Historical Work in the Colleges and Universities of Europe and America," in *Papers of the American Historical Association for the Year 1889*, Vol. IV (New York: Putnam's Sons, 1890), p. 57.

28. Temperley, *op. cit.*, pp. 6-7, 9, 22. Edward H. Carr notes that only in English-language countries is history excluded from science; see his *What Is History?* (New York: Alfred A. Knopf, 1962), pp. 70ff.

29. E. G. Bourne, "Leopold von Ranke," in *Annual Report of the American Historical Association for the Year 1896* (Washington, D.C.: Government Printing Office, 1897), pp. 65-80, especially 69-70.

30. *Loc. cit.*, p. 58.

31. Fueter, *op. cit.*, pp. 518, 522. For the view that these four historians represent "a central expression of romantic thought in America," see David Levin, *History as Romantic Art: Bancroft, Prescott, Motley, and Parkman* (Stanford, Calif.: Stanford University Press, 1959), p. 229.

32. Cf. Richard Hofstadter, *Social Darwinism in American Thought, 1860–1915* (Philadelphia: University of Pennsylvania Press, 1944. Rev. ed.,; New York: Braziller, 1955, 1959).

33. H. C. Carey, *Principles of Social Science* (3 vols.; Philadelphia: J. B. Lippincott and Company, 1858-60), I, 33, 35, 41.

34. Lester F. Ward, *Dynamic Sociology, or Applied Social Science, as based upon Statical Sociology and the Less Complex Sciences* (2 vols.; New York: D. Appleton and Company, 1883), I, pp. 20, 479, 503.

35. Donald E. Emerson, "Hildreth, Draper, and 'Scientific History,'" in *Historiography and Urbanization: Essays in American History in Honor of W. Stull Holt*, ed. Eric F. Goldman (Baltimore: Johns Hopkins University Press, 1941), pp. 139-70. See also Donald E. Emerson, *Richard Hildreth* (Baltimore: Johns Hopkins University Press, 1946), pp. 109ff.

36. John William Draper, *History of the Intellectual Development of Europe* (5th ed.; New York: Harper and Brothers, 1869), p. 621. In the Harper 1876 revised edition (2 vols.), I, iii.

37. *Papers of the American Historical Association for the Year 1886* (New York: Putnam's Sons, 1887), p. 8.

38. Herbert B. Adams, *The Study of History in American Colleges and Universities* (Bureau of Education Circular of Information No. 2 [Washington, D.C.: Government Printing Office, 1887]), pp. 175, 177, 179-80.

39. Cf. William H. Jordy, *Henry Adams: Scientific Historian* (New Haven: Yale University Press, 1952), pp. 3-4.

40. *Papers of the American Historical Association*, Vol. I (New York: Putnam's Sons, 1885), p. 483.

41. *Ibid.*, p. 483n.

42. E. G. Bourne, "Leopold von Ranke," *loc. cit.*, pp. 65-80.

43. William M. Sloane, "History and Democracy," *American Historical Review*, I (Oct., 1895), 1-23, especially 1, 16.

44. Henry Adams, *The Education of Henry Adams* (New York: Random House, 1931), p. 493.

45. To Francis Parkman, Dec. 21, 1884, in *The Selected Letters of Henry Adams,* ed. Newton Arvin (New York: Farrar, Straus and Young, 1951), pp. 86-87.

46. To Charles Milnes Gaskell, June 18, 1894, *loc. cit.,* p. 186.

47. "The Tendency of History," in *Annual Report of the American Historical Association for the Year 1894* (Washington, D.C.: Government Printing Office, 1895), pp. 17-23. This was a letter to the Secretary of the Association, Herbert B. Adams, which Henry Adams gave as his 1894 presidential address.

48. To Brooks Adams, Aug. 10, 1902, in *The Selected Letters of Henry Adams,* p. 237. See also Henry Adams, *The Degradation of the Democratic Dogma* (New York: Macmillan Company, 1896, 1919), p. v.

49. Brooks Adams, *The Law of Civilization and Decay: An Essay on History* (New York: Macmillan Company, 1896), pp. v, x-xi, 313-51,364.

50. Edward P. Cheyney, "Law in History," *American Historical Review,* XXIX (Jan., 1924), 231-48. The quotation is from p. 245. This was Professor Cheyney's presidential address before the American Historical Association in December, 1923.

51. For a recent and challenging criticism of Cheyney's "laws," see Warren B. Walsh, *Perspectives and Patterns: Discourses on History* (Syracuse: Syracuse University Press, 1962), ch. ii.

52. Ernest Cuneo, *Science and History* (New York: Duell, Sloan and Pearce, 1963), especially pp. 6, 206-30.

53. Various aspects of history, American and European, have been treated by John Higham, Leonard Krieger, and Felix Gilbert, *History* (Englewood Cliffs, N.J.: Prentice-Hall, 1965).

CHAPTER II

1. G. M. Trevelyan, "Stray Thoughts on History," in *This Is My Philosophy: Twenty of the World's Outstanding Thinkers Reveal the Deepest Meanings They Have Found in Life,* ed. Whit Burnett (New York: Harper and Brothers, 1957), pp. 95-103, especially 96.

2. James A. Froude, *Short Studies on Great Subjects* (New York: Scribner, Armstrong and Company, 1872), pp. 7, 21-22.

3. José Ortega y Gasset, *History as a System and Other Essays Toward a Philosophy of History* (New York: W. W. Norton Company, 1941, 1961), p. 203.

4. *War and Peace,* trans. Constance Garnett (unabridged; New York: The Modern Library, 1940[?]), pp. 774-76, 1127.

5. Samuel Rosenblatt, *The High Ways to Perfection of Abraham Maimonides,* Vol. II (Baltimore: Johns Hopkins University Press, 1938), p. 91. (Vol. I published by Columbia University Press, 1927.)

6. Tolstoy, *op. cit.,* p. 270.

7. Quoted by L. B. Namier, in *Avenues of History* (London: Hamish Hamilton, 1952), p. 6.

8. *The Portable Voltaire,* ed. Ben Ray Redman (New York: The Viking Press, 1961), p. 549.

9. K. B. Smellie, *Why We Read History* (London: Paul Elek, 1947), p. 7.

10. Kenneth Scott Latourette, "The Christian Understanding of History," *American Historical Review,* LIV (Jan., 1949), 259-76.

11. Karl Jaspers, *The Origin and Goal of History* (London: Routledge and Kegan Paul, 1953), pp. xv, 1, 265.

12. Pieter Geyl, "Toynbee's System of Civilizations," in *Toynbee and History: Critical Essays and Reviews,* ed. M. F. Ashley Montagu (Boston: Porter Sargent, Publisher, 1956), pp. 39-72, especially 43.

13. Toynbee, *op. cit.,* X, 3.

14. Cf. Shailer Mathews, *The Spiritual Interpretation of History.*

15. Ralph Linton, *The Study of Man: An Introduction* (student's ed.; New York: D. Appleton-Century Company, 1936), p. 489.

16. Thomas Carlyle, *On Heroes, Hero-Worship and the Heroic in History* (New York: Scribner's Sons, n.d. [published originally, 1841]), pp. 1, 184, 202, 237.

17. B. H. Lehman, *Carlyle's Theory of the Hero: Its Sources, Development, History and Influence on Carlyle's Work: A Study of a Nineteenth Century Idea* (Durham, N.C.: Duke University Press, 1928), p. 41.

18. Carlyle, *op. cit.,* p. 202.

19. Lehman, *op. cit.,* pp. 39ff.

20. To J. S. Mill, India House, 21 March 1841, in *Letters of Thomas Carlyle to John Stuart Mill, John Sterling and Robert Browning,* ed. Alexander Carlyle (New York: Frederick A. Stokes Company, 1923), p. 176.

21. Tolstoy, *op. cit.,* pp. 568ff.

22. Jacob Burckhardt, *Force and Freedom: Reflections on Freedom,* ed. James Hastings Nichols (New York: Pantheon Books, 1943), pp. 303, 345.

23. Seligman, *The Economic Interpretation of History* (2nd ed., rev.; New York: Columbia University Press, 1934 [published originally, 1902]), p. 97.

24. *The Hero in History: A Study in Limitation and Possibility* (New York: The John Day Company, 1943), p. 123.

25. Lee Benson, *Turner and Beard: American Historical Writing Reconsidered* (Glencoe, Ill.: The Free Press, 1960), p. 107.

26. Seligman, *op. cit.*, pp. 67, 159, 113-33.

27. Cf. Harold T. Parker, "Henri Sée (1864–1936)," in *Some Historians of Modern Europe: Essays in Historiography by Former Students of the Department of History of the University of Chicago*, ed. Bernadotte E. Schmitt (Chicago: University of Chicago Press, 1942), ch. xx, especially p. 464.

28. F. M. Powicke, *Modern Historians and the Study of History: Essays and Papers* (London: Odhams Press, 1955), p. 240.

29. Cf. *Capital, The Communist Manifesto, and Other Writings by Karl Marx*, ed. Max Eastman (New York: Random House, 1932), pp. 9-11, 318-19, 321. For an analysis of the Marxian interpretation of history, see Karl Federn, *The Materialist Conception of History* (London: Macmillan Company, 1939); Carl L. Becker, *Everyman His Own Historian: Essays in History and Politics* (New York: Appleton-Century-Crofts, 1935), pp. 113-31; and Herbert Butterfield, *History and Human Relations* (London: Collins, 1951), pp. 66-100.

30. Carl L. Becker, *How New Will the Better World Be? A Discussion of Post-War Reconstruction* (New York: Alfred A. Knopf, 1944), pp. 134-72; *Everyman His Own Historian*, pp. 113ff.; and *Detachment and the Writing of History: Essays and Letters of Carl L. Becker*, ed. Phil L. Snyder (Ithaca: Cornell University Press, 1958), p. 81.

31. Charles A. Beard, "Written History as an Act of Faith," *American Historical Review*, XXXIX (Jan., 1934), 219-29, especially 228.

32. Howard K. Beale, "Charles A. Beard: Historian," in *Charles A. Beard: An Appraisal*, ed. Howard K. Beale (Lexington: University of Kentucky Press, 1954), pp. 115ff. Professor Beard's reputation as an economic interpretationist derives mainly from his book *An Economic Interpretation of the Constitution of the United States* (New York: Macmillan Company, 1913). Beard believed that the Constitution was primarily an economic document and that it was framed and ratified chiefly by men who had interests in "money, public securities, manufactures, and trade and shipping." On the ratification of the Constitution, he found the line of cleavage between these interests and those of small farmers and debtors. These views have had able critics and defenders. See Bernard C. Borning, *The Political and Social Thought of Charles A. Beard* (Seattle: University of Washington Press, 1962), pp. 289-95; and Jennings B. Sanders, *A College History of the United States* (2 vols.; Evanston, Ill.: Row, Peterson and Company, 1962), I, 161-62.

33. Halvdan Koht, "The Importance of the Class Struggle in Modern History," *Journal of Modern History*, I (Sept., 1929), 353-60, and II (March, 1930), 61-64, especially 63.

34. Henry Thomas Buckle, *History of Civilization in England* (2nd ed., 2 vols.; New York: D. Appleton and Company, 1876).

35. New York: Houghton Mifflin, 1903, p. 226.

36. See Frederick J. Turner, "The West as a Field for Historical Study," in *Annual Report of the American Historical Association for the Year 1896* (Washington, D.C.: Government Printing Office, 1897), pp. 281-96, especially 284.

37. Seligman, *op. cit.*, pp. 135-36; Benson, op. cit., pp. 34, 90. Among other points, the Turner thesis includes the following: The correct viewpoint in American history is western, not eastern; the Atlantic coast was the frontier of Europe; the frontier became American as it advanced westward; free land, on whose outer edge the frontier lay, determined American development; the frontier advanced successively to the "Fall Line," the Alleghenies, the Mississippi, the Missouri, the 90th meridian, and to the Rockies; occupationally, there were frontiers of fur traders, farmers, miners, and cattlemen; the frontier encouraged democracy and nationalism, developed the powers of the national government, and Americanized the immigrants; American social life was continually reborn on the frontier, and from it the American intellect derived its chief characteristics, such as coarseness, inquisitiveness, restlessness, nervous energy, individualism, grasp of things material, and buoyancy. See Frederick J. Turner, *The Frontier in American History* (New York: Henry Holt and Company, 1920), ch. i; Ray A. Billington, *The American Frontier* (Washington, D.C.: American Historical Association, 1958); and Jennings B. Sanders, *A College History of the United States*, I, 291-92.

38. Thomas Babington Macaulay, *Critical, Historical, and Miscellaneous Essays and Poems* (3 vols.; New York: R. Worthington, n.d.), I, 271-72.

39. *The History of Herodotus*, trans. George Rawlinson, ed. Manuel Kornroff (New York: Tudor Publishing Company, 1956), pp. 1, 355, *et passim* .

40. A. L. Rowse, *The Use of History* (London: Hodder and Stoughton, 1946), pp. 86, 106.

41. Harold Temperley, *Selected Essays of J. B. Bury*, pp. 6-7, 9, 22.

42. H.[erbert] Butterfield, *The Whig Interpretation of History* (London: G. Bell and Sons, Ltd., 1959), pp. 91, 132.

43. Otis A. Pease, *Parkman's History: The Historian as Literary Artist* (New Haven: Yale University Press, 1953), pp. 80ff.

44. *Everyman His Own Historian*, p. 135.

45. To Mrs. Grattan Doyle, Dec. 9, 1935, in *An Historian's World: Selections from the Correspondence of John Franklin Jameson*, eds. Elizabeth Donnan and Leo F. Stock (Philadelphia: The American Philosophical Society, 1956), pp. 358-59.

46. Theodore Roosevelt, "History as Literature," *American Historical Review,* XVIII (April, 1913), 473-89, especially 476.

47. Quoted by J. Huizinga in "History and Changing Form," *Journal of the History of Ideas,* IV (April, 1943), p. 217.

48. *Ibid.*

49. Herbert Butterfield, *History and Human Relations,* pp. 232ff., 254.

50. Hegel, *Reason in History: A General Introduction to the Philosophy of History,* trans. Robert S. Hartman (New York: The Liberal Arts Press, 1953), p. 55.

51. Cf. James Westfall Thompson, *op. cit.,* II, 422-28.

52. Buckle, *op. cit.,* I, 166-67.

53. Oswald Spengler, *The Decline of the West,* trans. Charles Francis Atkinson, with notes (2 vols.; New York: Alfred A. Knopf, 1961 [published originally, 1926-28]); Toynbee, *op. cit.*

54. Kant, *On History,* trans. L. W. Beck, R. E. Anchor, and E. L. Fackenheim; ed. L. W. Beck (Indianapolis; The Bobbs-Merrill Co., 1963), pp. 11-26, especially p. 23.

55. William H. McNeill, *The Rise of the West: A History of the Human Community* (Chicago: University of Chicago Press, 1963), p. 806.

56. Jacques Pirenne, *The Tides of History* (New York: E. P. Dutton and Co., 1926), I, 9.

57. Thomas Carlyle, *English and Other Critical Essays* (New York: E. P. Dutton and Co., 1940), p. 86.

58. James Schouler, *Historical Briefs* (New York: Dodd, Mead and Co., 1896), p. 26.

CHAPTER III

1. M. C. D'Arcy, S.J., *The Meaning and Matter of History: A Christian View* (New York: Farrar, Straus and Cudahy, 1959), pp. 10-11, 11n.

2. Karl R. Popper, *The Open Society and Its Enemies,* pp. 11-12.

3. Karl R. Popper, *The Poverty of Historicism* (Boston: Beacon Press, 1957), pp. vii, x, 35-36.

4. See, for example, Charles A. Beard, "That Noble Dream," *American Historical Review,* XLI (Oct., 1935), 74-87.

5. Crane Brinton, *Ideas and Man: The Story of Western Thought* (Englewood Cliffs, N.J.: Prentice-Hall, 1950), pp. 493-94.

6. Dwight E. Lee and Robert N. Beck, "The Meaning of Historicism," *American Historical Review,* LIX (April, 1954), 568-77.

7. Warren B. Walsh, *Perspectives and Patterns: Discourses on History,* ch. i.

8. Morton White, *Social Thought in America: The Revolt Against Formalism* (Boston: Beacon Press, 1957 [published originally, 1947]), p. 12. For the view that modern historicism and relativism began to develop in the seventeenth century, see F. Smith Fussner, *The Historical Revolution: English Historical Writing and Thought, 1580–1640* (London: Routledge and Kegan Paul, 1962), pp. 318, 320.

9. Theodore Clarke Smith, "The Writing of American History in America, from 1884 to 1934," *American Historical Review,* XL (April, 1935), 439-49, especially 449.

10. Charles A. Beard, "That Noble Dream," *loc. cit.*

11. Statement is made by *Harvard Guide to American History,* eds. Oscar Handlin, *et al.* (Cambridge: Belknap Press of Harvard University Press, 1954), p. 19.

12. Max Farrand, *The Development of the United States from Colonies to a World Power* (Boston: Houghton Mifflin, 1918), p. ix.

13. Samuel Eliot Morison, "Faith of a Historian," *American Historical Review,* LVI (Jan., 1951), 261-75, especially 262-63.

14. Arthur M. Schlesinger, *New Viewpoints in American History* (New York: Macmillan Company, 1922), p. x.

15. Cf. *New York Times Magazine,* July 29, 1962, pp. 12ff., and August 12, 1962, p. 4.

16. Author's personal recollection of Professor Thompson's remarks made at a University of Chicago history alumni gathering.

17. Henry Charles Lea, "Ethical Values in History," *American Historical Review,* IX (Jan., 1904), 233-46, especially 234-37.

18. Cf. Joseph Ratner (ed.), *Intelligence in the Modern World: John Dewey's Philosophy* (New York: Random House, 1939), pp. 762ff.; John Dewey, *Experience and Nature* (Lasalle, Ill.: The Open Court Publishing Company, 1958 [published originally, 1925, 1929]), p. 15; Karl R. Popper, *The Open Society and Its Enemies,* pp. 388-89; Alfred North Whitehead. *Adventures of Ideas* (New York: Macmillan Company, 1956 [published originally, 1933]), p. 376.

19. Gordon G. Kaufman, *Relativism, Knowledge and Faith* (Chicago: University of Chicago Press, 1960), p. 3.

20. Charles A. Beard, "Written History as an Act of Faith," *American Historical Review,* XXXIX (Jan., 1934), 219-31, especially 225. The alleged discrepancies, inconsistencies, and contradictions in Beard's later philosophy as compared with his earlier, are discussed by Morton White, *op. cit.,* ch. xiv.

21. While Benedetto Croce and Wilhelm Dilthey (1833-1911) were relativists, Heinrich Rickert (1863-1936) and Ernst Troeltsch (1865-1923) were counter-relativists. Dilthey tried to reconcile the absolute with belief in relativism. Sociologist Karl Mannheim (1893-1947) has been called a relativist by Maurice Mandelbaum, an identification not admitted by Mannheim. Cf. Maurice Mandelbaum, *The*

Problem of Historical Knowledge: An Answer to Relativism (New York: Liveright Publishing Company, 1938), pp. 40, 67, 156. See also Karl Mannheim, *Freedom, Power, and Democratic Planning* (New York: Oxford University Press, 1950), pp. xiii-xiv; and Gerhard Masur, "Wilhelm Dilthey and the History of Ideas," *Journal of the History of Ideas*, XIII (Jan., 1952), p. 96.

22. Helmut Schoeck and James W. Wiggins, *Relativism and the Study of Man* (New York: Van Nostrand, 1961), pp. 175-96.

23. Toynbee, *op. cit.*, XII, 651-57; Pieter Geyl, *Debates with Historians* (New York: Philosophical Library, 1956), p. 177.

24. *Thus Spake Zarathustra*, trans. Thomas Common (New York: Random House, n.d.), p. xiv.

25. Toynbee, *op. cit.*, X, 139.

26. Cf. Crane Brinton, *Ideas and Men: The Story of Western Thought*, p. 496.

27. Michael Oakeshott, "The Activity of Being a Historian," in *Historical Studies: Papers Read Before the Second Irish Conference of Historians*, ed. T. Desmond Williams (New York: Hillary House, 1958), pp. 1-19, especially 18-19.

28. *The Philosophy of History*, p. 16.

29. Pieter Geyl, *Encounters in History*. Cleveland: World Publishing Company, 1961), p. 357.

30. Edward P. Cheyney, "Law in History," *loc. cit.*, especially p. 247.

31. William M. Sloane, "History and Democracy," *American Historical Review*, I (Oct., 1895), 1-23, especially 5.

32. Quoted by Ferdinand Schevill, *Six Historians*, p. 130.

33. Jacob Burckhardt, *Judgments on History and Historians*, trans. Harry Zohn, Intro. by H. Trevor-Roper (Boston: Beacon Press, 1958), p. xi.

34. Oakeshott, *loc. cit.*, pp. 7-9, 18-19.

35. J. H. Hexter, *Reappraisals in History* (Evanston, Ill.: Northwestern University Press, 1961), pp. 1-13.

36. Ibn Khaldûn, *The Muqaddimah*, I, lxviii, 56, 58.

37. Boston: Ginn and Company, 1925, p. iii.

38. James Harvey Robinson and Charles A. Beard, *The Development of Modern Europe: An Introduction to the Study of Current History* (2 vols.; Boston: Ginn and Company, 1907-08), I, iii-iv.

39. Herman Ausubel, *Historians and Their Craft: A Study of Presidential Addresses of the American Historical Association, 1884–1945* (New York: Columbia University Press, 1950), pp. 359, 361. Professor Samuel Flagg Bemis, in his presidential address before the Association, December, 1961, said that history "fortifies our judgment in dealing with problems of the present and measuring our hopes for

the future—I will not say in shaping the future" ("American Foreign Policy and the Blessings of Liberty," *American Historical Review,* LXVII [Jan., 1962], 291).

40. "The Study of History in Schools, Being the Report to the American Historical Association by the Committee of Seven," in *Annual Report of the American Historical Association for the Year 1898* (Washington, D.C.: Government Printing Office, 1898), pp. 427-564, especially 439-40.

41. "The Study of History in Secondary Schools," in *Annual Report of the American Historical Association for the Year 1910* (Washington, D.C.: Government Printing Office, 1911), pp. 209-42. The quotation is from p. 240.

42. Charles M. Andrews, "Should Recent European History have a place in the College Curriculum," *Annual Report of the American Historical Association for the Year 1899* (Washington, D.C.: Government Printing Office, 1900), pp. 539-48. The quotation is from p. 542.

43. Edward Channing, Albert B. Hart, and Frederick J. Turner, *Guide to the Study and Reading of American History* (rev. ed.; Boston: Ginn and Company, 1912 [published originally, 1896]), p. 6.

44. Frederick J. Turner, "The West as a Field for Historical Study," in *Annual Report of the American Historical Association for the Year 1896,* pp. 281-96. The quotation is from p. 283.

45. W. H. Walsh, "The Limits of Scientific History," in *Historical Studies, III: Papers Read Before the Fourth Irish Conference of Historians,* ed. James Hogan (New York: Hillary House, 1961), pp. 45-57, especially 45-46, 57.

46. Raymond Aron, *Introduction to the Philosophy of History: An Essay on the Limits of Historical Objectivity* (Boston: Beacon Press, 1961 [French ed., 1938]), p. 157.

47. [Friedrich] Meinecke, "Historicism and Its Problems," in *The Varieties of History from Voltaire to the Present,* ed. Fritz Stern (New York: Meridian Books, 1956), p. 272.

48. *Theory and Practice in Historical Study: A Report of the Committee on Historiography* (New York: Social Science Research Council, 1946), pp. 136, 137n. Beard's historical concepts changed from time to time during his career. See Morton White, *op. cit.,* ch. xiv, *et passim.* See also Bernard C. Borning, *The Political and Social Thought of Charles A. Beard.*

49. Marcus G. Singer and Robert B. Ammuman (eds.), *Introductory Readings in Philosophy* (New York: Scribner's Sons, 1962), p. 131.

50. John Stuart Mill, *Essays on Political Culture,* ed. Gertrude Himmelfarb (Garden City, N.Y.: Doubleday and Company, 1962), p. 423.

51. Patrick Gardiner, *The Nature of Historical Explanation* (London: Geoffrey Cumberlege, Oxford University Press, 1952), pp. 70-71, 109; Geoffrey Barraclough, "The Historian in a Changing World," in *The Philosophy of History in Our Time: An Anthology,* ed. Hans Meyerhoff (Garden City, N.Y.: Doubleday, 1959), p. 32.

52. Marc Bloc, *The Historian's Craft,* trans. Peter Putnam (New York: Knopf, 1959), pp. 43, 190, 194.

53. Buckle, *op. cit.,* I, 599ff. "Like the ordinary man," says Carr, the historian "believes that human actions have causes which are in principle ascertainable. History, like everyday life, would be impossible if this assumption were not made" (*What Is History?,* p. 125).

54. Frederick J. Teggart, *The Processes of History* (New Haven: Yale University Press, 1918), p. 52.

55. Lee Benson, *Turner and Beard: American Historical Writings Reconsidered,* p. 34, *et passim;* Seligman, *op. cit.,* pp. 135-36.

56. Walter Prescott Webb, *The Great Plains* (Boston: Ginn and Company, 1931), pp. 184ff.

57. Seligman, *op. cit.,* pp. 67, 113, 127-33.

58. Richard B. Schlatter, "The Problem of Historical Causation in Some Recent Studies of the English Revolution," *Journal of the History of Ideas,* IV (June, 1943), 349-67, especially 366-67.

59. Nathan Rotenstreich, *Between Past and Present: An Essay on History* (New Haven: Yale University Press, 1958), p. 318.

60. Auguste Comte, *A General View of Positivism,* trans. J. H. Bridges (New York: Robert Speller and Sons, 1957), p. 62.

61. Heinrich Rickert, *Science and History: A Criticism of Positivist Epistemology,* trans. George Reisman, ed. Arthur Goddard (New York: D. Van Nostrand, 1962), pp. 88, 91.

62. Friedrich Meinecke, "Historicism and Its Problems," *loc. cit.,* pp. 268-76.

63. [Samuel Johnson], *Thoughts on the Late Transactions Respecting Falkland's Islands* (2nd ed.; London: Printed for T. Cadell, in the Strand, 1771), p. 33. This work, included in a volume identified as *Johnson's Tracts,* was used in the Henry E. Huntington Library, San Marino, California.

64. Richard Pares, *The Historian's Business and Other Essays,* eds. R. A. and Elisabeth Humphreys (Oxford: At the Clarendon Press, 1961), pp. 7, 9. Cf. Carr, *What Is History?,* p. 113.

65. See Dana C. Munro, "War and History," *American Historical Review,* XXXII (Jan., 1927), 219-31, especially 229.

66. Carl Becker, "Everyman His Own Historian," *loc. cit.,* 221-22.

67. Perez Zagorin, "Carl Becker on History. Professor Becker's Two Histories: A Skeptical Fallacy," *American Historical Review,* LXII (Oct., 1956), 1-11.

68. Cf. Leo Gershoy, "Zagorin's Interpretation of Becker: Some Observations," *American Historical Review,* LXII (Oct., 1956), 12-17.

69. Charles A. Beard, "Written History as an Act of Faith," *loc. cit.,* p. 219-31. This paper was Professor Beard's presidential address before the American Historical Association, December, 1933.

70. "The practical requirements which underlie every historical judgment give to all history the character of 'contemporary history . . .' " (*History as the Story of Liberty,* p. 19).

71. *Detachment and Writing of History: Essays and Letters of Carl L. Becker,* ed. Phil L. Snyder, pp. 41-64. Important for the thinking of both Becker and Beard, is Cushing Strout's *The Pragmatic Revolt in American History: Carl Becker and Charles Beard* (New Haven: Yale University Press, 1958).

72. Cf. Conyers Read, "The Social Responsibilities of the Historian," *American Historical Review,* LV (Jan., 1950), 275-85, especially 280.

73. Erich Kahler, *The Meaning of History* (New York: George Braziller, 1964), p. 181.

74. Beard, "Written History as an Act of Faith," *loc. cit.,* p. 226.

75. Cf. Henry Osborn Taylor, "Continuities in History," *American Historical Review,* XLIV (Oct., 1938), 1-19, especially 4.

76. *Detachment and Writing of History: Essays and Letters of Carl L. Becker,* p. 24.

77. Allen Johnson, *The Historian and Historical Evidence* (New York: Scribner's Sons, 1926), p. 160. Ernst Cassirer has said that self-effacement by the historian cannot produce objectivity; rather, he says, it would deprive him "of the very instrument of all historic thought" (*An Essay on Man: An Introduction to a Philosophy of Human Culture* [New Haven: Yale University Press, 1944], p. 187).

CHAPTER IV

1. Andrew McFarland Davis, writing over three-quarters of a century ago, lamented the lack of detailed histories of Southern campaigns against the Indians during the Revolutionary War. His explanation of why this was so, is revealing: "At the time when the centennial anniversaries of these events might fitly have been celebrated by the publication of such original material as could be found, there was not the same disposition in the South to be grateful for the results of the Revolutionary War as prevailed in the North." That is, the South only recently having lost her "revolution" against the national government was little interested in American national history. See Justin Winsor (ed.), *Narrative and Critical History of America* (8 vols.; Boston: Houghton Mifflin, 1884-89), VI, 678.

2. Motley to his Mother, Feb. 9, 1861, in *The Correspondence of John Lothrop Motley,* ed. George W. Curtis (2 vols.; London: John Murray, 1889), I, 357-58.

3. Cf. Francis Newton Thorpe, "American History in Schools, Colleges, and Universities," in Herbert B. Adams, *The Study of History in American Colleges and Universities,* p. 229.

4. James Harvey Robinson, "The Newer Ways of Historians," *American Historical Review,* XXXV (Jan., 1930), 245-55, especially 252.

5. Cf. Richard W. Sterling, *Ethics in a World of Power: The Political Ideas of Friedrich Meinecke* (Princeton: Princeton University Press, 1958), pp. 153, 156-57.

6. Robert Cruden, *James Ford Rhodes: The Man, the Historian, and His Work with a Complete Bibliography of the Writings of James Ford Rhodes* (Cleveland: The Press of Western Reserve University, 1961), pp. 150-56ff.

7. Cf. Burleigh T. Wilkins, *Carl Becker: A Biographical Study in American Intellectual History* (Cambridge: Massachusetts Institute of Technology Press and Harvard University Press, 1961), pp. 125-35.

8. Sterling, *op. cit.,* p. 5.

9. A. Robert Caponigri, *History and Liberty: The Historical Writings of Benedetto Croce* (London: Routledge and Kegan Paul, 1955), p. 263.

10. Cf. Richard H. Bauer, "Veit Valentin 1885-1947," in *Essays on Eminent Europeans: Some 20th Century Historians,* ed. S. William Halperin (Chicago: University of Chicago Press, 1961), pp. 103-41, especially 130ff.

11. Charles Francis Adams, "An Undeveloped Function," in *Annual Report of the American Historical Association for the Year 1901* (2 vols.; Washington, D.C.: Government Printing Office, 1902), I, 49-93.

12. The report is contained in *Annual Report of the American Historical Association for the Year 1898* (Washington, D.C.: Government Printing Office, 1899), pp. 427-564. Pages 499-564 are Appendixes I-VIII; quotations are from pp. 439-40.

13. The report is contained in *Annual Report of the American Historical Association for the Year 1910* (Washington, D.C.: Government Printing Office, 1911), pp. 209-42. The quotation is from p. 240.

14. Channing, Hart, and Turner, *op. cit.,* p. 6. Professor William E. Dodd of the University of Chicago saw in wide diffusion of knowledge of American history among his countrymen hope for American democracy's survival. See Charlotte Watkins Smith, *Carl Becker: On History and the Climate of Opinion* (Ithaca: Cornell University Press, 1956), pp. 192, 208.

15. Rolla M. Tryon, *The Social Sciences as School Subjects* (Report of the Commission on the Social Studies, Part XI; New York: Scribner's Sons, 1935), p. 76.

16. Eggleston to Adams, April 14, 1898, *Historical Scholarship in the United States, 1876–1901: As Revealed in the Correspondence of Herbert B. Adams,* ed. W. Stull Holt (Baltimore: Johns Hopkins University Press, 1938), pp. 253-54.

17. H. B. Adams, *The Study and Teaching of History* (Richmond, Va.: Whittet and Shepperson, 1898), pp. 15-16.

18. Robert S. Fletcher, "The Heroic Age of the Social Sciences," *Indiana Magazine of History,* XLV (Sept., 1949), 221-32.

19. James Harvey Robinson, *The New History: Essays Illustrating the Modern Historical Outlook* (Springfield, Mass.: The Walden Press, 1958 [published by Macmillan Company, 1912]), pp. 24, 70-100. See also Robinson's *The Mind in the Making: The Relation of Intelligence to Social Reform* (New York: Harper and Brothers, 1921, 1931), pp. 5, 171ff.

20. Isaiah Berlin, *Historical Inevitability* (London: Oxford University Press, 1954, 1959), pp. 51, 76-79. Professor Page Smith says that "history is not a scientific enterprise but a moral one" (*The Historian and History* [New York: Alfred A. Knopf, 1964], p. 229).

21. C. V. Wedgwood, *Truth and Opinion: Historical Essays* (London: Collins, 1960), pp. 42-43.

22. Marie Collins Swabey, *The Judgment of History* (New York: Philosophical Library, 1954), pp. 16, 113, 172.

23. Herbert Butterfield, *History and Human Relations* (London: Collins, 1951), pp. 101-30.

24. Whitehead, *Adventures of Ideas,* p. 346.

25. *Intelligence in the Modern World: John Dewey's Philosophy,* ed. Joseph Ratner, pp. 1-36.

26. Quoted by B. A. Hinsdale in *How to Study and Teach History with Particular Reference to the History of the United States* (New York: D. Appleton and Company, 1894), p. 6.

27. Quoted *ibid.,* p. 5n.

28. *Annual Report of the American Historical Association for the Year 1898,* pp. 439-40. Italics supplied by the author.

29. "Law in History," *loc. cit.,* pp. 231-48. See also Edward P. Cheyney, *Law in History and Other Essays* (New York: Alfred A. Knopf, 1927).

30. Froude, *op. cit.,* pp. 22-23.

31. J. B. Bury, *The Idea of Progress: An Inquiry into Its Origin and Growth* (New York: Macmillan Company, 1932), pp. 4, 335, 344.

32. Lea, "Ethical Values in History," *loc. cit.*

33. *Ibid.,* p. 236.

34. Oakeshott, "The Activity of Being an Historian," *loc. cit.*, pp. 17-19.

35. Toynbee, *op. cit.*, VIII, 272-313, especially 288-92; XII, 596-97, 624-28, 664-69. See also Pieter Geyl, "Toynbee's System of Civilization," and "Toynbee as Prophet," in *Toynbee and History: Critical Essays and Reviews*, ed. M. F. Ashley Montagu, pp. 39-72, 360-77, especially 362, 371; Abba Eban, "The Toynbee Heresy," *loc. cit.*, pp. 320-37.

36. In a recent critical review of a Toynbee book, Crane Brinton also puts Toynbee beyond the historian's pale. "Clearly," says Brinton, Toynbee "gives the public something the professional historian does not give him" (*American Historical Review*, LXVIII [April, 1963], 758).

37. See the appreciative article, without author's name, entitled "John Franklin Jameson," *American Historical Review*, XLIII (Jan., 1938), 243-52.

38. *An Historian's World: Selections from the Correspondence of John Franklin Jameson*, eds. Elizabeth Donnan and Leo F. Stock, pp. 152-53, 201-02.

39. To Theodore Francis Green, April 28, 1937, *loc. cit.*, p. 365.

40. To William E. Dodd, May 12, 1920, *loc. cit.*, p. 250.

41. To Theodore Francis Green, April 28, 1937, *loc. cit.*, p. 365.

42. To Mrs. Grattan Doyle, Dec. 9, 1935, *loc. cit.*, pp. 358-59.

43. J. Franklin Jameson, *The History of Historical Writing in America* (New York: Argosy Antiquarian Press, Ltd., 1961 [published originally, Boston: Houghton Mifflin, 1891]), pp. 93-95.

44. *Ibid.*, pp. 132-33.

CHAPTER V

1. Hugh Murray, F.R.S.E., *The United States of America; Their History from the Earliest Period; Their Industry, Commerce, Banking Transactions, and National Works; Their Institutions and Character, Political, Social, and Literary; With a Survey of the Territory, and Remarks on the Prospects and Plans of Emigrants;* with illustrations of the natural history by James Nicol; portraits and other engravings by Jackson (3 vols.; Edinburgh: Oliver and Boyd; London: Simpkin, Marshall and Company, 1844), I, 400.

2. *Ibid.*, p. 400.

3. John W. Draper, *History of the Intellectual Development of Europe.*

4. Arthur O. Lovejoy, *Essays in the History of Ideas* (Baltimore: Johns Hopkins University Press, 1948), pp. 10-13.

5. Alexis Carrel, *Man the Unknown* (New York: Harper and Brothers, 1935, 1939), pp. 47-50.

6. Toynbee, *op. cit.,* IX, 193-203.

7. Pitirim A. Sorokin, "Toynbee's Philosophy of History," in *Toynbee and History,* ed. M. F. Ashley Montagu, pp. 172-87, especially 178. See also Pieter Geyl, *Use and Abuse of History* (New Haven: Yale University Press, 1955), pp. 62-63.

8. Robert K. Merton, Leonard Broom, and Leonard S. Cottrell, Jr. (eds.), *Sociology Today: Problems and Prospects* (New York: Basic Books, 1960). See also Joseph B. Gittler (ed.), *Review of Sociology: Analysis of a Decade* (New York: John Wiley and Sons, 1957); and Paul F. Lazarsfeld and Morris Rosenberg (eds.), *The Language of Social Research: A Reader in the Methodology of Social Research* (Glencoe Ill.: The Free Press, 1955).

9. See Merton, Broom, and Cottrell, *op. cit.,* Pt. III; Gittler, *op. cit.,* pp. 520-30; and Leonard Broom and Philip Selznick, *Sociology: A Text with Adapted Readings* (Evanston, Ill.: Row, Peterson and Company, 1956), ch. xiv. Sketches of the life and work of Durkheim, Pareto, and Weber, by C. Bouglé, Talcott Parsons, and Hans Speier, respectively, may be found in the *Encyclopedia of Social Sciences,* V, 291-92; XI, 576-78; and XV, 386-89.

10. *Culture and Behavior: The Collected Essays of Clyde Kluckhohn,* ed. Richard Kluckhohn (New York: The Free Press of Glencoe, 1962), chs. xvi-xvii.

11. Cf. Kimball Young, *Social Psychology* (New York: F. S. Crofts and Company, 1946), chs. x, xiii-xiv, xviii, xxi.

12. David Riesman, *Individualism Reconsidered and Other Essays* (Glencoe, Ill.: The Free Press, 1954), p. 308.

13. *Ibid.,* pp. 305-08.

14. Cf. Richard Pares, *The Historian's Business and Other Essays,* pp. 24-25.

15. *The Basic Writings of C. G. Jung,* ed. Violet Staub de Laszlo (New York: Random House, 1959), pp. 183-285, *et passim.*

16. Goodwin Watson, "Clio and Psyche: Some Interrelations of Psychology and History," *The Cultural Approach to History,* ed. for the American Historical Association by Caroline F. Ware (New York: Columbia University Press, 1940), p. 34. See also Franz Alexander, "Psychology and the Interpretation of Historical Facts," *loc. cit.,* pp. 48-57.

17. See Brooks Adams' Introduction to Henry Adams, *The Degradation of the Democratic Dogma* (New York: Macmillan Company, 1919), pp. vi, 10, 83-84.

18. Page Smith, *John Adams* (2 vols.; Garden City, N.Y.: Doubleday, 1962), I, 70-71. For studies of Woodrow Wilson and certain other historical personages, but not including an Adams, which suggest uses to which psychology may be put by the historian, see Bruce

Mazlish, *Psychoanalysis and History* (Englewood Cliffs, N.J.: Prentice-Hall, 1963).

19. Aleš Hrdlička, "Origin of the American Aborigines," in *The Golden Age of American Anthropology*, eds. Margaret Mead and Ruth L. Bunzel (New York: George Braziller, 1960), pp. 432-38.

20. Alfred Cobban, "History and Sociology," *Historical Studies, III: Papers Read Before the Fourth Irish Conference of Historians*, ed. James Hogan, p. 7.

21. Morton White, *op. cit.,* p. 12.

22. For Vitalis, see Léopold Delisle, "Notice sur Orderic Vital," in *Orderici Vitalis Angligenae, Coenobii Uticensis Monachi, Historiae Ecclesiasticae*, ed. Augustus Le Prevost (5 vols.; Paris: 1838-55), V, 1-cvi; Charles H. Haskins, *The Normans in European History*, pp. vii-viii, 174, 180-83, 258; and Ordericus Vitalis, *The Ecclesiastical History of England and Normandy*.

23. The early seminars at Johns Hopkins were directed by Dr. Austin Scott, assistant to George Bancroft. Sessions were held at the Maryland Historical Society and the Peabody Institute in Baltimore. See Herbert B. Adams, *The Study of History in American Colleges and Universities*, pp. 171ff.

24. Herbert B. Adams, "The Teaching of History," in *Annual Report of the American Historical Association for the Year 1896*, pp. 245-63, especially 247.

25. Ephraim Emerton, "The Requirements for the Historical Doctorate in America," in *Annual Report of the American Historical Association for the Year 1893* (Washington, D.C.: Government Printing Office, 1894), 79-90, especially 81-83.

26. Cf. John Higham, "The Rise of American Intellectual History," *American Historical Review*, LVI (April, 1951), 453-71, especially 458-59, 463-67.

27. Cf. Roy F. Nichols, "Postwar Reorientation of Historical Thinking," *American Historical Review*, LIV (Oct., 1948), 78-89, especially 79-80.

28. Cf. Higham, *loc. cit.*

29. Boyd C. Shafer, "Men Are More Alike," *American Historical Review*, LVII (April, 1952), 593-612.

30. Leonard Krieger, "The Horizons of History," *American Historical Review*, LXIII (Oct., 1957), 62-74, especially 73-74.

31. Ralph Linton, *The Cultural Background of Personality* (New York: D. Appleton-Century Company, 1945), pp. xiii-xix.

32. William L. Langer, "The Next Assignment," *American Historical Review*, LXIII (Jan., 1958), 283-304, especially 303.

33. Cf. Lester F. Ward, *Dynamic Sociology, or Applied Social Science, as based upon Statical Sociology and the Less Complex Sci-*

ences; and Thorstein Veblen, *The Theory of the Leisure Class: An Economic Study in the Evolution of Institutions* (New York: Macmillan Company, 1899).

34. Karl Mannheim, *Freedom, Power, and Democratic Planning,* pp. xiii-xv.

35. See especially, Dexter Perkins, "We Shall Gladly Teach," *American Historical Review,* LXII (Jan., 1957), 291-309; and Dexter Perkins and John L. Snell, *The Education of Historians in the United States* (New York: McGraw-Hill, 1962), chs. iv, viii-ix.

36. James Schouler, *Historical Briefs* (New York: Dodd, Mead and Company, 1896), pp. 22-33.

CHAPTER VI

1. Carl Becker, "The Reviewing of Historical Books," in *Annual Report of the American Historical Association for the Year 1912* (Washington, D.C.: Government Printing Office, 1914), p. 133.

2. Samuel Eliot Morison, "Faith of a Historian," *loc. cit.,* p. 263.

3. Allen Johnson, *The Historian and Historical Evidence,* unpaged Preface.

4. Louis Gottschalk, "A Professor of History in a Quandary," *American Historical Review,* LIX (Jan., 1954), 273-86, especially 274.

5. Richard Pares, *The Historian's Business and Other Essays,* p. 3.

6. *Historical Scholarship in the United States, 1876–1901: As Revealed in the Correspondence of Herbert B. Adams,* ed. W. Stull Holt, p. 8. This work will hereafter be cited as "Herbert B. Adams, *Correspondence.*"

7. George E. Howard to Herbert B. Adams, May 30, 1883, Herbert B. Adams, *Correspondence,* p. 65.

8. John Herman Randall, Jr., *Nature and Experience: Essays in Naturalism and in the Theory of History* (New York: Columbia University Press, 1958), p. 27.

9. Parkman to Mary Dwight Parkman, [1852], in *Letters of Francis Parkman,* ed. Wilbur R. Jacobs (2 vols.; Norman: University of Oklahoma Press, 1960), I, 99.

10. Of this amount, $60,000 represented estimated value of Adams' labor for twelve years, and $20,000 represented cash outlays. Adams said he did not welcome a large return from his work, since this would put historical writing on a level with magazine writing. See Ernest Samuels, *Henry Adams: The Middle Years* (Cambridge: Belknap Press of Harvard University Press, 1958), pp. 338-39.

11. Even in 1841, Bancroft received $4,250 in royalties. But his library alone cost $9,000, and this was only one of many expenses. Prescott, after some discouragement at the outset of his publishing career, achieved huge success: in one four-month period, Harper's

sold 12,000 copies of his *Conquest of Mexico,* and in one six-month period, he received from his various histories, $17,000. See Russel B. Nye, *George Bancroft: Brahmin Rebel* (New York: Alfred A. Knopf, 1944), pp. 120-21; and *The Literary Memoranda of William Hickling Prescott,* ed. C. Harvey Gardiner (2 vols.; Norman: University of Oklahoma Press, 1961), II, 118, 224.

12. Cf. M. A. DeWolfe Howe (ed.), *The Life and Letters of George Bancroft* (2 vols.; New York: Scribner's Sons, 1908), II, 260-62, 286-87.

13. Motley to Dr. O. W. Holmes, May 16, 1858, in *The Correspondence of John Lothrop Motley,* ed. George W. Curtis, I, 223.

14. Raymond C. Miller, "James Ford Rhodes," in *The Marcus W. Jernegan Essays in American Historiography,* ed. William T. Hutchinson (Chicago: University of Chicago Press, 1937), p. 174.

15. In the late 1870's, the combined income of Adams and his wife was $20,000–$25,000 a year. By the late 1880's, Adams, now a widower, had double this amount (Ernest Samuels, *op. cit.,* pp. 29, 221, 317, 424-25).

16. Cf. Jennings B. Sanders, "Evolution of Accreditation," in *Accreditation in Higher Education,* ed. Lloyd E. Blauch (Washington, D.C.: Government Printing Office, 1959), pp. 12-13.

17. Dexter Perkins and John L. Snell, *The Education of Historians in the United States,* pp. 116, 118, 139.

18. John S. Bassett to [Herbert B.] Adams, Jan. 16, 1896, Herbert B. Adams, *Correspondence,* p. 242.

19. Marian Churchill White, *A History of Barnard College* (New York: Columbia University Press, 1954), quoting, p. 48.

20. Carl Becker, *Everyman His Own Historian,* pp. 191-232, especially 194. As a historian, Becker showed little interest in geography, maps, and statistics, all of which were of much concern to Turner. Cf. Charlotte Watkins Smith, *op. cit.,* pp. 196-97.

21. Arthur M. Schlesinger, Jr., *The Age of Roosevelt: The Politics of Upheaval* (Boston: Houghton Mifflin, 1960), p. 451; Alpheus T. Mason and William M. Beaney, *The Supreme Court in a Free Society* (Englewood Cliffs, N.J.: Prentice-Hall, 1959), p. 1.

22. R. F. Arragon, "Techniques and Place of History in General Education," *Journal of General Education,* April, 1950, p. 186.

23. Richard Pares, *op. cit.,* p. 2.

24. Theodore Roosevelt, "History as Literature," *American Historical Review,* XVIII (April, 1913), 473-89, especially 479-80.

25. Cf. Herbert B. Adams, *Correspondence,* p. 90n. Wilson later formed a more favorable opinion of Adams.

26. Adams to Daniel Coit Gilman, July 3, 1882, Herbert B. Adams, *Correspondence,* p. 55.

27. Boyd C. Shafer, "The Historian in America," *The Southwestern Historical Quarterly*, LX (Jan., 1957), 381-86, especially 384.

28. Johan Huizinga, *Men and Ideas: History, the Middle Ages, the Renaissance*, trans. James S. Holmes and Hans van Marle (New York: Meridian Books, 1959), pp. 19-20.

29. With the Sir Lewis Namier school of British historians apparently in mind, Herbert Butterfield foresees a time when historians representing a particular point of view may all be "reviewing one another and standing shoulder to shoulder" to stifle dissent. See Herbert Butterfield, *George III and the Historians* (rev ed,; New York: Macmillan Company, 1959), p. 8. See also Henry R. Winkler, "Sir Lewis Namier," *Journal of Modern History*, XXXV (March, 1963), 1-19.

30. Thomas Babington Macaulay, *Critical, Historical, and Miscellaneous Essays and Poems*, I, 515-33, especially 516.

31. Quoted by Albert Bushnell Hart, "Imagination in History," *American Historical Review*, XV (Jan., 1910), 228.

32. Carl Becker, "The Reviewing of Historical Books," *loc. cit.*, pp. 129-36.

33. *Toynbee and History*, ed. M. F. Ashley Montagu; Toynbee, *op. cit.*, vol. xii, pp. 573-657; Pieter Geyl, *Use and Abuse of History*, pp. 65-67. When Sir Ernest Barker taunts him for having in his Index only one-sixth as much space for England as for Egypt, Toynbee deftly uses the criticism as a basis for expressing regret that he had so underrated Egypt and over-rated England. He says that only his Western and English bias could have led him to believe that England was entitled to as much as one-sixth the space allotted Egypt—that one-sixtieth the space for England would have been more equitable. He almost apologizes for being an Englishman. (Toynbee, *loc. cit.*)

34. Henri Pirenne, "What Are Historians Trying to Do?" in Meyerhoff, *The Philosophy of History in Our Time*, p. 94.

35. G. J. Renier, *History: Its Purpose and Method* (Boston: Beacon Press, 1950), p. 32.

36. Sir Charles Oman, *On the Writing of History* (New York: E. P. Dutton and Company, [1939?]), pp. 297, 300.

37. Adams to Elizabeth Cameron, Dec. 12-13, 1891, in *The Selected Letters of Henry Adams*, ed. Newton Arvin, p. 158.

CHAPTER VII

1. For the view that no national character exists and that the concept of one is "a defunct myth," see W. P. Metzger in *Generalization in the Writing of History: A Report of the Committee on Historical Analysis of the Social Science Research Council*, ed. Louis Gottschalk (Chicago: University of Chicago Press, 1963), p. 77.

2. Cf. Edward W. Chester, *Europe Views America: A Critical Evaluation* (Washington, D.C.: Public Affairs Press, 1962), ch. iii.

3. Richard Pares, *War and Trade in the West Indies, 1739–1763* (Oxford: At the Clarendon Press, 1936), p. 467.

4. Frederick J. Turner also identified as American traits, coarseness, inventiveness, inquisitiveness, restlessness, and possession of unusual nervous energy. See above, ch. ii, n37. Among helpful works on American traits and character are: Frederick Lewis Allen, *The Big Change: America Transforms Itself* (New York: Harper and Brothers, 1947); R. L. Bruckberger, *Image of America* (New York: The Viking Press, 1959); Edward M. Burns, *The American Idea of Mission: Concepts of National Purpose and Destiny* (New Brunswick, N.J.: Rutgers University Press, 1957); Henry S. Commager, *The American Mind: An Interpretation of American Thought Since the 1880's* (New Haven, Conn.: Yale University Press, 1950); Peter F. Drucker, *The New Society: The Anatomy of the Industrial Order* (New York: Harper and Brothers, 1949); Marshall Fishwick, "The Big Search for America," *Saturday Review*, Aug. 16, 1958, pp. 8ff.; Eric Goldman, *The Crucial Decade: America, 1945–1955* (New York: Alfred A. Knopf, 1956); Clinton Rossiter, *Conservatism in America* (New York: Alfred A. Knopf, 1955); André Siegfried, *America at Mid-Century* (New York: Harcourt, Brace and Company, 1955).

5. The role of "abundance" in shaping American cultural traits has been developed by David M. Potter in his *People of Plenty: Economic Abundance and the American Character* (Chicago: University of Chicago Press, 1954).

6. Max Weber, *The Protestant Ethic and the Spirit of Capitalism*, trans. Talcott Parsons (New York: Scribner's Sons, [1930]).

7. Frederick Merk, *Manifest Destiny and Mission in American History: A Reinterpretation* (New York: Alfred A. Knopf, 1963), p. 27. In his conclusion that the American people never subscribed to the doctrine of "Manifest Destiny" to the extent that is popularly supposed, it may be that Professor Merk has overstressed the continental and hemispheric connotations of the doctrine. Most Americans probably have conceived of the doctrine in the more restricted sense of expansion to the Pacific. In this context, it may have had a wider appeal than Professor Merk suggests.

8. G. M. Trevelyan, "Stray Thoughts on History," in *This Is My Philosophy*, ed. Whit Burnett, p. 98.

9. C. Vann Woodward, *Reunion and Reaction: The Compromise of 1877 and the End of Reconstruction* (Boston: Little, Brown and Company, 1951), p. 118, citing (n50) a letter from William E. Chandler to Hayes, Jan. 13, 1877, in the Hayes Papers.

10. Cf. Talcott Parsons, review of James Willard Hurst's *Law and Social Process in United States History*, in *Journal of the History of Ideas*, XXIII (Oct.-Dec., 1962), 561.

11. Leonard M. Marsak (ed.), *French Philosophers from Descartes to Sartre* (Cleveland and New York: World Publishing Company, 1961), p. 241.

12. Cf. Archibald Henderson, *George Bernard Shaw: Man of the Century* (New York: Appleton-Century-Crofts, 1956), p. 265.

13. Roscoe Pound, *New Paths of the Law* (Lincoln: University of Nebraska Press, 1950), pp. 51-52. Of relevance to the theme discussed in this section is J. George Harrar's "New Ventures for Private Philanthropy," *New York Times Magazine,* June 9, 1963, pp. 29ff.

14. Edward H. Carr, *What Is History?* (New York: Alfred A. Knopf, 1962), pp. 146-58.

15. Morris R. Cohen, *The Meaning of Human History* (LaSalle, Ill.: The Open Court Publishing Company, 1947), p. 107.

16. James Schouler, *Historical Briefs,* p. 25.

17. Henry David Thoreau, *Walden* (New York: W. W. Norton and Company, 1951), p. 67.

18. See Roosevelt's statement in *Foreign Relations of the United States, Diplomatic Papers: The Conferences at Malta and Yalta, 1945* (Washington, D.C.: Government Printing Office, 1955), p. 923.

19. John K. Galbraith, *The Affluent Society* (Boston: Houghton Mifflin, 1958), pp. 255, 315-33. See also Irving Kristol, "Is the Welfare State Obsolete?" *Harper's Magazine,* June, 1963, pp. 39-43, especially, 42.

20. On frustrations that result for Americans from their country's power-position in the world, see Reinhold Niebuhr, *The Irony of American History* (New York: Scribner's Sons, 1952), pp. 134, 140ff.

21. Robert L. Heilbroner, *The Future as History: The Historic Currents of Our Time and the Direction in Which They Are Taking America* (New York: Harper and Brothers, 1959, 1960), p. 14.

22. Oswald Spengler, *op. cit.*

23. Arnold J. Toynbee, *op. cit.*

24. A. L. Kroeber, *The Nature of Culture* (Chicago: University of Chicago Press, 1952), pp. 402-08.

25. Bertrand Russell, *New Hopes for a Changing World* (New York: Simon and Schuster, 1951), p. 6.

26. Lewis Mumford, *In the Name of Sanity* (New York: Harcourt, Brace and Company, 1954), pp. 154-55, 166-68, 178ff.

27. Auguste Comte, *A General View of Positivism,* pp. 3-7, 50-62, 355, 360, 364.

28. John U. Nef, *Cultural Foundations of Industrial Civilization* (Cambridge: At the University Press, 1958), p. 154.

29. Karl R. Popper, *The Open Society and Its Enemies.*

30. John Gardner, "The Ever-Renewing Society," *Saturday Review,* Jan. 5, 1963, pp. 92-95.

31. Carl L. Becker, *How New Will the Better World Be?* (New York: Alfred A. Knopf, 1944), pp. 134-72.

32. Charles A. Beard, "Written History as an Act of Faith," *loc. cit.*, p. 228.

33. Roscoe Pound preferred the term "service state" to "welfare state," since he felt that welfare was implicit in our constitutional system. See his *New Paths of the Law*, pp. 51-52. Dean Pound was one of America's most acute thinkers on the relationship of law to social change and on the need for "social engineering." Cf. his *The Formative Period of American Law* (New York: Peter Smith, 1950); *An Introduction to the Philosophy of Law* (New Haven: Yale University Press, 1922); and *Interpretations of Legal History* (New York: Macmillan Company, 1923), ch. vii. Similar views have been expressed by James Willard Hurst (see below, n46).

34. Roberto Michel's *First Lectures in Political Sociology*, trans. Alfreda Grazia (Minneapolis: University of Minnesota Press, 1949), pp. 135, 137.

35. Karl Jaspers, *The Future of Mankind* (Chicago: University of Chicago Press, 1961), pp. 293-94. This work was published originally in Munich in 1958, under the title *Die Atombombe und die Zukunst des Menschen*.

36. David M. Potter, *People of Plenty*, p. x.

37. Professor Beard's historical writings were extensive, and there is a growing bibliography of writings on these. See Bernard C. Borning, *The Political and Social Thought of Charles A. Beard*, pp. 257-89 (writings by Beard), 289-95 (writings about Beard).

38. For Hurst and Pound references, see n13, n33, n46, this chapter.

39. F. Smith Fussner, *The Historical Revolution*, p. 319.

40. See John Higham, "Intellectual History and Its Neighbors," *Journal of the History of Ideas*, XV (June, 1954), 339-47; Rowland Berthoff, "The American Social Order: A Conservative Hypothesis," *American Historical Review*, LXV (April, 1960), 495-514; and Dixon Ryan Fox, "A Synthetic Principle in American Social History," *American Historical Review*, XXXV (Jan., 1930), 256-66. Also see Fox, *Ideas in Motion* (New York: D. Appleton-Century Company, 1935), pp. 77-97; and Joseph Dorfman, *The Economic Mind in American Civilization* (5 vols.; New York: The Viking Press, 1946-59).

41. Cf. Edwin E. Aubrey, "Social Psychology as Liaison between History and Sociology," *American Historical Review*, XXXIII (Jan., 1928), 257-77, especially 273-74. See also Richard L. Means, "Sociology and History: A New Look at Their Relationships," *American Journal of Economics and Sociology*, XXI (July, 1962), 285-98. On the problem of generalization, see Louis Gottschalk (ed.), *Generalization in the Writing of History: A Report of the Committee on Histor-*

ical Analysis of the Social Science Research Council. Professor William B. Willcox, in a review article on this book ("The Historian's Dilemma," *Journal of Modern History,* XXXVI, June, 1964, p. 180) says that if teachers and textbook writers confined themselves to evidence, "they would have almost nothing worthwhile to say," and that "we have to be inaccurate in order to teach at all."

42. Cf. H. A. Hodges, *The Philosophy of Wilhelm Dilthey* (London: Routledge and Kegan Paul, 1952), pp. 174-75.

43. Cf. Herbert W. Schneider, *A History of American Philosophy* (New York: The Liberal Arts Press, 1957), p. 334; Morton G. White, "The Revolt Against Formalism in American Thought in the Twentieth Century," *Journal of the History of Ideas,* VIII (April, 1947), 131-32; Edwin E. Aubrey, *loc. cit.* Justice Holmes said: "The first requirement of a sound body of law is, that it should correspond with the actual feelings and demands of the community, whether right or wrong" (O. W. Holmes, Jr., *The Common Law* [Boston: Little, Brown and Company, 1881], p. 41).

44. Henry Thomas Buckle, *op. cit.,* I, 174-75. Despite numerous examples of selfishness and authoritarianism that can be cited in American history, any attempt to make a "myth" of the role of liberty in that history seems completely to misunderstand its meaning.

45. Cf. Dexter Perkins, *The American Approach to Foreign Policy* (rev. ed.; Cambridge: Harvard University Press, 1962), pp. 72-76.

46. Cf. James Willard Hurst, *Law and Social Process in United States History* (Ann Arbor: University of Michigan Law School, 1960), pp. 43-44, *et passim; The Growth of American Law: The Law Makers* (Boston: Little, Brown and Company, 1950), pp. 11, 13; and *Law and the Conditions of Freedom in the Nineteenth-Century United States* (Madison: University of Wisconsin Press, 1956), ch. ii.

47. Rowland Berthoff, *loc. cit.*

48. On the theme of physical mobility, see George W. Pierson, " 'A Restless Temper . . .,' " *American Historical Review,* LXIX (July, 1964), 969-89.

49. Harold J. Ruttenberg, *Self-Developing America* (New York: Harper and Brothers, 1960), pp. 7, 42ff., 96-97, 133 ff. Pertinent to this human rights survey is Merle Curti, "The Democratic Theme in American Historical Literature," *Mississippi Valley Historical Review,* XXXIX (June, 1952), 3-28. This *Review* has been succeeded by *The Journal of American History,* and the Mississippi Valley Historical Association by The Organization of American Historians.